"Philip De Courcy throws a life preserver out to all of us who are drowning in the everyday struggles of life. Philip weaves together stories from his own life with the eternal truth of God's Word. Each chapter shows you a new way to *Take Cover* when the waves roll in and you feel yourself starting to sink. I hope you'll buy two copies—one to read yourself and one to share with a friend. It's that good."

—Dr. Ray Pritchard, president, Keep Believing Ministries

"So many live in fear, and that includes many Christians who battle anxiety and live in the dread that terrible things may happen at any time. This of course is no way to live and winning this spiritual battle is essential for the believer's personal well-being. Phillip De Courcy offers vibrant solutions as to how we can overcome in life by finding shelter in the promises and provisions of our great God. *Take Cover* will equip and encourage you from God's Word and challenge you to live in the victory Jesus gives all who trust in Him. Living under God's protection is what this extraordinary book is about and I wholeheartedly endorse its author and message."

—Dr Jack Graham, pastor, Prestonwood Baptist Church, Plano Texas

"Why do so many people try so hard to keep God out of their thoughts and conversations? We know, of course, that in the mind of the typical unbeliever, any mention of God is perceived as threatening. And no wonder. It is true on the one hand that our God is a consuming fire. It is a fearful thing to fall into the hands of the living God. Scripture expressly says fear of God is the beginning of wisdom. On the other hand, for those who believe, there is no more comforting presence than God himself. In fact, His perfect righteousness is the basis for His grace and mercy—not just His wrath. His mercies are over all His works. He Himself is our stronghold—our shield and our strength. He gives grace and peace and everlasting comfort to all those who seek their refuge in Him. Scripture is full of rich promises and reassuring comforts like those that apply to every believer. But peace in the midst of earthly suffering doesn't come spontaneously to the believer. Our prayers, our worship, a Bible-centered worldview, and the armor God supplies are all essential instruments by which we must avail ourselves of the shelter God provides. I know of no better, clearer exposition of these themes than Philip De Courcy's excellent book, *Take Cover*. Here you will be reminded and instructed how to hide yourself in the tender love of God, where you can always find rest for your soul. I love this theme, and I am profoundly grateful for Pastor De Courcy's insightful exposition of it. I highly recommend this book."

—John MacArthur, pastor-teacher, Grace Community Church,
Sun Valley, CA, president, The Master's University and Seminary,
voice of the daily *Grace to You* radio broadcast

"Every faithful Christian knows from Scripture and from experience that the walk of faith thrusts us into spiritual warfare. And yet, although we live in the midst of constant cosmic strife—wrestling "against the spiritual forces of evil in the heavenly places"—God promises His children that His peace, which surpasses human understanding, will keep our hearts and minds. How is that possible? And how can the Christian who is caught in the strife of spiritual conflict or earthly vexations lay hold of that peace? Philip De Courcy has clear, simple answers to that question in this delightfully readable digest of some of Scripture's finest promises. You will love *Take Cover*—and I think you'll greatly benefit from its simple, biblical wisdom."

—Phil Johnson, executive director, *Grace to You* radio broadcast

TAKE COVER

FINDING PEACE IN GOD'S PROTECTION

PHILIP De COURCY

TAKE COVER

FINDING PEACE IN GOD'S PROTECTION

PHILIP De COURCY

SALEMBOOKS
an imprint of Regnery Publishing

Regnery® is a registered trademark of Salem Communications Holding Corporation

Salem Books™ is a trademark of Salem Communications Holding Corporation

Cataloging-in-Publication data on file with the Library of Congress

ISBN: 978-1-62157-804-8
Ebook ISBN: 978-1-62157-846-8

Library of Congress Cataloging-in-Publication Data

Published in the United States by
Salem Books, an imprint of
Regnery Publishing
A Division of Salem Media Group
300 New Jersey Ave NW
Washington, DC 20001
www.Regnery.com

Manufactured in the United States of America

2018 Printing

Books are available in quantity for promotional or premium use. For information on discounts and terms, please visit our website: www.Regnery.com

To Rich Riddle

and

John Van Wingerden

Friends in life and partners in ministry

CONTENTS

IN THE LINE OF FIRE

Everyone who is a man of God has omnipotence
as his guardian, and God will sooner empty
heaven of angels than leave a saint without defense

Charles Haddon Spurgeon

Before becoming a pastor, I served several years as an active-duty police officer in the reserve forces of the Royal Ulster Constabulary (RUC) in Northern Ireland. If you know anything about Northern Ireland during the late 1960s and forward, you know it was anything but an oasis of peace. For some forty years Northern Ireland endured virtual war, known as the Troubles. Yet it was during those turbulent times God planted the seeds for the message of this book as He taught me how to find security in Him while I navigated life on the frontlines of the civil conflict in Northern Ireland.

In his book, *Turning Mountains into Molehills,* Warren Wiersbe tells the story of a young soldier on furlough. Just prior to being shipped out to the battlefield, he decided to pay a visit to his grandfather who was housebound and afflicted with a debilitating disease. Both were believers, and he knew there'd be much to gain by spending a few hours with this wise and godly man to help prepare him for what lay ahead.

As the two men talked, the young soldier shared his concerns about military service and particularly his fear of death. He asked, "Grandfather, please pray for me that I'll have the courage to die?" The grandfather looked at him through eyes revealing the pain he was bearing and replied, "I will, my son, and please pray for me that I'll have the courage to live."[1]

The grandfather's prayer offers us a powerful insight and would remind us it takes courage to live as well as die, sometimes more. For the Christian, death is not the worst thing. Because of Christ's substitutionary death for our sins and triumphant resurrection, death for the believer opens the door to an eternity with God and pleasures forever more (Phil. 1:21; Psa. 16:11). As the apostle Paul declared, to be with Christ is "far better" (Phil. 1:23). But to live day after day, year after year, facing uncertainty, or trapped in a body wrecked with pain or surrounded by harsh and unyielding circumstances is often much harder to face with courage.

Take Cover is a book about what it takes to find courage to live—to take cover in the Lord, especially in such uncertain and perilous times. How do we take cover in the promises and presence of God? What does it mean to be secure? By way of introduction, I want to share four lessons I learned during my days as a RUC officer in Northern Ireland.. God wants us to take cover in Him and to find our security in Him, His providence (Rom. 8:28), presence (Heb. 13:5), promises (2 Peter 1:4), and protection (Psa. 46:1). Each of these lessons will form the substance of what I believe God wants for His children as I expound on them in the coming chapters.

As mentioned earlier, for more than six years, from 1982 to 1988, I served as an active-duty reserve officer in the RUC in north Belfast. At its peak, the RUC had 8,500 officers with a further 4,500 members of the RUC Reserve. During the civil unrest, more than 300 members of the police service were murdered. In addition to the fatalities, almost 9,000 officers were injured in community conflict and terrorist attacks, perpetrated mostly by the provisional Irish Republican Army (IRA). At that time, to be an officer in the RUC was to fulfill one of the most dangerous policing roles in the world. In fact, in 1983, Interpol declared Northern Ireland as the most dangerous policing role in the world; El Salvador came in second.

During my time in our station on the Antrim Road in north Belfast, several officers were shot at and wounded. Rocket-propelled grenades hit our station on a couple occasions. We foiled bombing attempts on the station, and one of our cadre, Sergeant Donald Guthrie was shot dead driving into the station by the IRA on June 23, 1987. I remember the drizzly day we walked solemnly behind his coffin draped in the Union Jack, to the cries of his wife and family. That was Northern Ireland on a constant, almost daily basis.

Yet, God gave me the courage to live. As a Christian police officer, my faith in Christ made a huge difference in how I responded to the constant danger, seen and unseen. As a justified man I sought to live by faith in the promise of God's constant presence and protection (Gal. 2:20; Heb. 10:38). I've reflected many times on my days there and I how I found peace in Northern Ireland amid all the killing and terror. That's where and when I learned many valuable lessons, the greatest being that security is not the absence of danger but the presence of God. The crucible of the conflict in Northern Ireland proved to be the furnace in which I forged a strong faith in God. Even though I carried a gun on and off duty and though I wore body armor while patrolling the streets of Belfast, my ultimate security lay in God as my shield and defense (Psa. 3:3; 28:7). So, as we begin this book, let me outline what God taught me during those trying times in Northern Ireland with emphasis on the sense of security I found in knowing my times were in God's hands (Psa. 31:15). The best security a man or woman can find is faith in God.

1. I LEARNED TO USE THE CONSTANT THREAT OF DEATH AS A MOTIVATION TO LIVE WISELY AND WELL.

One thing about being a RUC officer was you were never safe even when you were off duty. You were just as likely to be killed out of uniform as in. Think about that? The threat posed by the IRA and other violent groups was always present. Many officers were assassinated at home, out shopping, or going to church or blown up sitting in their own car. The threat of death was present and imminent. I felt just as exposed after my shift was finished as when I was on patrol. I carried a concealed 9-mm pistol wherever I went; I checked under my car in the mornings for booby traps, watched my company, and varied my routes while driving.

The threat of death was a twenty-four-hour, seven-day-a-week reality. In fact, I recall in one of my early antiterrorist training classes with the RUC and British army, we were shown a bone-chilling video titled, "You Could Be Next." In that video, we learned about various IRA tactics, including under-car booby traps, pressure plates, all manner of improvised explosive devices, and other strategies for killing us. The purpose of the video was no doubt to scare, inform, and put us on alert. It worked well, I left that training session more aware than ever before of my precarious position and need for vigilance.

The thought of death encroached upon everything I did, and yet God taught me to use that almost suffocating sense of death as a means and motivation to live wisely and well. If my life were to be cut short, I needed to make every day count (Eph. 5:15–17; James 4:13–17).

God ministered to me through several verses reminding me to repeatedly consider the end of life, allowing the approach of death to bring about a new beginning of obedience and deeper spiritual accountability in my life. Verses such as Ecclesiastes 7:1–4, Psalm 90:12, and Psalm 39:4 reminded me the thought of death can act as elixir for better living. As the Puritans advocated, meditation upon the day of one's death is good, it taught me to treasure time, prioritize relationships, hold material possessions lightly, keep short accounts with God, and greatly rejoice in Jesus Christ as the One who said, "I am the resurrection and the life" (John 11:25–26).

Living under the shadow of death reminded me and reminds us to live life passionately, wisely, and purposefully. There's an old Irish expression: *Live today as if it were your last day, because some day it will be.* That's good, isn't it? When you live with that truth in view, the small stuff stays small, the important things remain a priority, heaven becomes closer, and faith in the eternal God becomes central to life (Psa. 90:1–2).

The lexicographer and wit Samuel Johnson famously said, "When a man knows he is about to be hanged in a fortnight, it concentrates his mind wonderfully." The thought of death certainly shaped my thinking and focused my life. The shadow of death helps us better appreciate and apportion life. We tend to run from the thought of death, as a RUC officer, that was impossible and ultimately proved to be a good thing. Let us not run from the thought of death, let the thought of death cause us to step back and run from sin and shallowness in life.

We can take cover in the fact death will not have the final say; Jesus has defused death of its power and menace, bringing life and the prospect of immortality to our journey on earth (2 Tim. 1:10). The Christian can face death unafraid and unbowed.

2. I LEARNED TO LEAVE THE FINAL ACT OF JUSTICE AND JUDGMENT TO GOD.

One of the things I struggled greatly with during my time in the police was the arrogance of evil men and the fact that in many of their cases justice was never serviced. Their crimes went unpunished, their murders went unsolved, and bad guys went unpunished. During the dark days of the Troubles, it often seemed as though truth was on the scaffold and evil on the throne. Apologists for the IRA, like Sein Fein, could be heard on the nightly news. Prosecutions failed because witnesses were intimidated. The widows of soldiers and policemen and the orphans of terrorism seemed to go unnoticed. My struggle of faith was with the prosperity of the wicked and the apparent absence of God's judgment against evil. At times it seemed God was an absentee landlord in relation to the world and its woes.

You may feel that same sense of injustice. How is it the dope dealer, the gang leader, the terrorist mastermind seem to go unchecked? How is it the abuser lives life unmolested? How is it the merchants of death do not fear for their own lives? How is it those who continually ignore

God's righteous ways seem to be ignored by God? Where is God's just anger toward the unjust? Why do the unrighteous go unpunished?

These were my questions, but in time they were answered in my reading of Psalm 37 and 73. Both these Psalms deal with the prosperity of the wicked and the need for the believers to hold on to their faith in the final judgment of God against evil and the evildoer (Psa. 37:1–6, 9–17; 73:16–20). These Scriptures promise God will awake in judgment against the wicked, the end of the wicked is horrible and their punishment sure. The Bible wants us to know the righteous will come out on top. There is a higher court of justice that will right the wrongs. It has been well said, "The wheels of God's justice may grind slowly, but they do grind exceedingly small." Vengeance is God's, and He will repay the evil that molests us, frustrates us, and vexes our righteous souls (Rom. 12:19; Psa. 11:4–7; 2 Thess. 1:3–10).

I took cover in verses such as those when I was tempted to become bitter and doubt the goodness and holiness of God. Scripture reminded me the scales of justice would someday be balanced in favor of the righteous.

Pastor and author Steve Brown writes about a time when he was driving and noticed one of the most beat-up cars he'd ever seen on the road. It was riddled with dents, the windscreen was cracked, the doors were being held shut with bailing wire, the paint was faded and beginning to flake, and the muffler was touching the ground sending sparks in every direction. But the most interesting thing about the car however was the bumper sticker, which read, "This is Not an Abandoned Car."[2]

On many a day, just like you, I look out on our world and wonder how it could ever have gotten so bad. How long will evil continue to triumph? And it's in those times God reminds me through His Word, "This is Not an Abandoned World." I love that thought. In the end, Jesus and justice will reign. Evil will be judged, the righteous will be rewarded, and the wicked will be punished. In the end, it will be worth it to be counted among the righteous. Don't become lawless. Don't allow bitterness to take root. Keep your faith in God. Leave the final act of justice and judgment to God (Rev. 22:12–13, 20–21).

3. I LEARNED GOD IS NOT THE ENEMY OF MY ENEMIES FOR GOD IS NOT EVEN THE ENEMY OF HIS ENEMIES.

To switch gears, one of the most amazing things I encountered during my days as a police officer in Northern Ireland was the all-encompassing, wondrous power of the gospel to change lives (Rom. 1:16). As Paul notes in his letter to the Romans, "where sin abounded, grace abounded much more" (Rom. 5:20). Along with others I saw men of bloodshed be made clean through the blood of Christ, and men who stoked hatred become peacemakers having themselves made peace with God through faith in Christ (Rom. 5:1; Matt. 5:9). Terrorists on both the Catholic and Protestant sides of the conflict were transformed by the grace of God into new creatures in Christ (2 Cor. 5:17).

It was marvelous to behold. It's astonishing to see men of violence become peaceful, men full of hatred become loving, men who advocated death become preachers of the life-giving Gospel of Jesus Christ. The God who saved the thief-cum-terrorist by Jesus's side on the cross did it many more times during the conflict in Northern Ireland (Luke 23:39–43).

I witnessed firsthand the amazing nature and transforming power of God's grace while still in the police and preparing for ministry at the Irish Baptist College in Belfast. One of the guys I sat beside in class and befriended was a man named Billy McCurry. To his former colleagues in the Ulster Volunteer Force, a Loyalist terrorist group, he was known as "Chips" McCurry. Billy McCurry was a former gunman, who at the age of seventeen, murdered a man to avenge his father's killing by the IRA. Yet amazingly, following his arrest and incarceration, Billy McCurry found Christ during his time in the maximum-security Maze prison. Following his release Billy sensed a growing call to prepare himself for the ministry of pastoring and preaching and so enrolled in the Irish Baptist College where I first met him. Today Billy faithfully and fruitfully pastors Aughton Baptist Church in England. Imagine that, the active duty policeman and the ex-terrorist studying theology side by side at the Irish Baptist College in Belfast. Only God and only the Gospel of Jesus Christ can do that!

Billy is a trophy to God's amazing grace and a wonderful reminder that God has saved and does save the worst sinners (1 Tim. 1:12–17). God is a friend to sinners. Yes, God will judge the unrepentant wicked, but He is quick to forgive those who turn from their wickedness and place their trust in His Son (Isa. 55:6–7). In the midst of life's horrors and hurts we can take cover in the glorious truth that God can turn bad men into good Christian men.

The late Lutheran pastor Martin Niemoller who spent eight years in a Nazi concentration camp for his opposition to Hitler famously said, "It took a long time for me to understand that God is not the enemy of my enemies. God was not even the enemy of God's enemies." The book of Romans teaches us when we were God's enemies we were reconciled to God through the death of his Son (Rom. 5:6–11). It was in a war-torn place like Northern Ireland I learned that. The grace that saves and keeps a policeman, who was once God's enemy, is the same grace that touches and transforms the worst terrorists, who were God's and man's enemy.

4. FINALLY, I LEARNED DURING MY DAYS IN THE POLICE IN NORTHERN IRELAND THAT GENUINE SECURITY IS NOT FOUND IN THE ABSENCE OF DANGER BUT IN THE PRESENCE OF GOD.

Given the daily threat of assassination, you can imagine I took my personal security seriously. I did all within my power to protect myself. My trust in God did not alleviate me of my responsibility concerning my physical welfare. Like those in Nehemiah's day, I prayed to God and kept my eyes wide open for danger (Neh. 4:9). Like those in Oliver Cromwell's Parliamentary Army, "I trusted God and kept my powder dry." In the face of constant danger, I trusted my training, I used common sense, I altered my driving habits, I kept my police life as hidden as possible, and I carried my service pistol on me whenever I went. Yet, in taking every precaution I was fully aware of my vulnerability. There was a nagging feeling of insecurity, of living life looking over my shoulder, wondering if death was but a footstep behind me. I was not blind to the fact the terrorist always had the element of surprise, and a well-executed attack would most likely result in my death.

I watched my mother's hair go gray from worrying about me during my police years, wondering if I'd come home safely each time I went out on patrol. She often stayed up until I was safely in bed, despite the fact I was a twenty-two-year-old man. Her heart would skip a beat each time radio or TV newsflashes announced incoming reports of the injury or death of another police officer. The reality of the danger and the accompanying sense of insecurity took its toll on all of us. We all struggled in the battle between fear and faith.

God desires we live in confidence not fear (2 Tim. 1:7; Psa. 27:1–3). And confidence biblically speaking is not to be found in the absence of danger but in the presence of God.

As mentioned earlier the greatest lesson I learned during my time in the RUC Reserve was I needed to find my sense of security in God. In life danger and death are inescapable realties; a man's days are few and full of trouble (Job 14:1). You may run from death and danger, but you cannot hide from them. That is why we must not try to run from them, but turn and face them in the sure confidence God is near and will not forsake us (Psa. 145:18; Heb. 13:5). This was the secret to Joshua's strength and success in the face of great obstacles (Josh. 1:8–9). This was the secret to Paul's strength and steadfastness in the face of opposition (2 Tim. 4:16–18). This was the secret to Joseph's faith, love, and hope in the face of betrayal and hardship (Gen. 39:2–3, 21–23). As John Wesley said on his deathbed, "Best of all God is with us."

Many people are tempted to run and hide, to endlessly search for some far-off place where no threats exist. But that is a futile notion, a pipe dream, a nonstarter in a fallen world. There is not a square inch of this planet not disrupted or corrupted by sin and sinners. Heaven is the only place where perfect peace is to be found and where no threats exist (Rev. 21:1–4). Therefore, we need to learn that running from evil gets us nowhere.

Consider these words from Psalm 55:

> My heart is severely pained within me, and the terrors of
> death have fallen upon me. Fearfulness and trembling have
> come upon me, and horror has overwhelmed me. So I said,
> Oh that I had wings like a dove! I would fly away and be at
> rest. Psalm 55:4–7

Such sentiment is widely expressed by many of us today. If we could only fly away from it all. But there is no running from life with all its attendant problems, illnesses, and threats. Life is not about God sheltering us from life's hurt, rather it is about God sustaining us in the midst of them. This is to be seen in David who wrote Psalm 55 during a distressing period in his life when he responds by casting his burden on the Lord and then walking away in complete peace (Psa. 55:22–23). God does not remove the burden but sustains David under it. You see life is not about running away from evil but about God delivering us in the midst of evil (Matt. 6:13; 2 Tim. 4:16–17). God did not deliver Daniel from the lion's den but sustained him in it (Dan. 6:18–23), God did not deliver Daniel's friends from the fiery furnace but sustained them in it (Dan. 3:19–23), and God did not deliver Jesus from the cross but sustained him for it (Luke 22:39–46). It's the abiding, presiding, and providing presence of God that turns the tide in our hearts (Psa. 91:1–2). That's what this book is all about. Security is not the absence of danger, but the presence of God, the presence of God to save, strengthen, sweeten, succor, and sustain the people of God.

I was able to survive six years in the most dangerous policing role in the world at the time protected by that truth. I had my moments, I was scared, and I am not ashamed to admit that, but I was able to manage my fear and live courageously. Remember, courage is not the absence of fear but the ability to act despite your fears. As a policeman who was always in the crosshairs of a terror threat, I was able to keep calm and carry on by taking cover in the promise of God's presence while in the presence of my enemies (Psa. 23:5). I reminded myself often as we left through the gates of Antrim Road Police station to go on patrol that I lived, as did Job, between the hedges of God's protective presence and providence (Job 1:9–10). To get to me, the IRA would have to first go through God's will for my life. That kind of thinking and theology was my best weapon in fighting fear.

This sense of security and protective peace is something the world cannot give or understand (John 14:27; Phil. 4:6–7). Armed with the truth God is with us, we are well able to face our foes courageously and face our fears calmly. According to the Bible, if God is for us it does not matter who or what is arrayed against us (Rom. 8:32).

The great Confederate general Thomas "Stonewall" Jackson, and one of my heroes, got his name from his fearless engagement of the enemy. During one battle where his men were retreating under withering enemy fire, Jackson sat erect on his horse unperturbed amid the danger. One retreating soldier was heard to say, "There stands Jackson as a stonewall." That is how he got his name, but where did he get his courage? Thomas "Stonewall" Jackson got his courage from his faith in God's presence and providence. He once answered a question concerning his courage in these words, "My religious belief teaches me to feel as safe in battle as in bed."[3]

Love that! Stonewall Jackson is reminding us once again that security is not the absence of danger but the presence of God. The God who is sovereign over life stands by our side within life giving us a sense of peace in the face of death and danger. In the following chapters, you will discover eight principles for finding peace and security in the promises, provisions, and presence of God. Your family needs this. You need this. Your neighbor needs this. Our country needs this.

Take your time reading each chapter. Look up for yourself the Bible passages I include to illustrate each point. And most of all, ask the Lord to give you otherworldly peace, a peace that will allow you to live defiantly, victoriously, and joyfully in this dangerous world as a testimony to Jesus Christ, the Prince of Peace (Isa. 9:6).

That kind of peace was exhibited by the great preacher Chrysostom who remained defiant in the face of Roman threats. Listen as R. Kent Hughes describes the scene:

> When Chrysostom was brought before the Roman emperor, the emperor threatened him with banishment if he remained a Christian. Chrysostom replied, "Thou canst not banish me, for this world is my Father's house. "But I will slay thee," said the emperor. "Nay, thou canst not," said the noble champion of the faith, "for my life is hid with Christ in God." "I will take away thy treasures." "Nay, but thou canst not, for my treasure is in heaven and my heart is there." "But I will drive thee from man, and thou shalt have no friend left." "Nay, thou canst, for I have a friend in heaven from whom thou canst not separate me. I defy thee, for there is nothing that thou canst do to hurt me."[4]

In a world riddled with fear, swimming in anxiety and swamped by threatening trends from the Middle East to China, the Christian alone has the best chance of surviving the madness with an unshakable faith in God and His Son, Christ Jesus. Like Chrysostom, we need not allow ourselves to be bullied out of our faith or hope. Why? Because since nothing threatens God, nothing threatens the lives of those who make God their refuge and take cover in the promise of His presence and protections (Psa. 46:1). The Christian is immortal until God says otherwise.

CHAPTER 1

GET ON YOUR KNEES
TAKING COVER IN A LIFE GUARDED BY GOD'S PEACE THROUGH PRAYER

*You can do more than pray after you have prayed,
but you cannot do more than pray until you
have prayed*

S. D. Gordon

I n 1992, at the invitation of a young man in my church I boarded a British Army Puma helicopter out of Enniskillen in Northern Ireland to make the short but dangerous trip to the joint police and army base at Crossmaglen in South Armagh, an IRA stronghold. Because of the dangers inherent in this region to British security forces, it was nicknamed "Bandit Country." It was so bad the safest way in was by helicopter.

As we touched down and deplaned, we found ourselves opposite a large gable wall inside the heavily fortified station. The high protective structure bore the emblems of the Royal Ulster Constabulary and the British regiment serving alongside the police at that time. What caught my eye was what was written above the emblems, the words of Bobby McFerrin's song so popular in 1988, *Don't Worry, Be Happy*. I think

1

the hope was the words of that song might help put our minds at ease as we went boots down in bandit country.

I glanced again at the words, *Don't Worry, Be Happy*; they struck me as rather hollow and more psychological mumbo-jumbo than genuine solace for troubled minds. The combined reality of sparse barracks, tough living conditions, and the constant IRA threat just outside the gates, gave each soldier and police officer plenty to worry about and little about which to feel happy.

A couple of days after I returned home from my brief excursion into Crossmaglen, the raw reality of that terrorist threat surfaced as news broke of a shooting there. It was later confirmed a young police officer I talked to during my visit to the base was shot dead by an IRA sniper. I'll never forget the feelings of despair and dread that came over me. As I reflected upon my visit among those brave young men defending Northern Ireland's border, the remembrance of those words on the gable wall, *Don't Worry, Be Happy*, seemed only to mock that young man's death.

Let's be honest, it's hard to sing with any real belief or gusto songs such as *Don't Worry Be Happy* when they are set against the background noise of gunfire, explosions, and the weeping of those hurt by violence.

Almost without exception, nightly news broadcasts and daily online outlets continually stream graphic images from around the world of endless natural disasters, terrorist attacks, atrocities by radical Islam, and the upsetting plight of Middle East refugees fleeing war zones with little more than the clothes on their backs.

Mass shootings are on the increase and we wonder if we're safe to attend outdoor concerts or participate in public worship. Additionally, our own American society is being besieged by an unruly faction of angry, irrational protestors who care little for law and order and even less about the value of human life and property. All this conspires to trouble our minds and overwhelm our hearts with anxiety and fear.

Yet, it's into the chaos and alarm of our times God offers through His Son, Jesus Christ, the promise of peace surpassing human comprehension, the kind of peace that allows us to enjoy a little bit of the hush of heaven on earth. A perfect peace for an imperfect world as promised in Isaiah 26:3.

Writing around AD 61 during his first imprisonment in Rome, the apostle Paul called on the Philippians to turn their panic into prayer and then watch as God transformed their concerns into calm. In his letter to the Philippians he wrote these incomparable words:

> Be anxious for nothing, but in everything by prayer and sup-plication, with thanksgiving, let your requests be made known to God; and the peace of God, which surpasses all under-standing, will guard your hearts and minds through Christ Jesus.
>
> Philippians 4:4–7

As Paul writes this prescription for peace, it is worth noting the great apostle has taken his own medicine. Despite his own circumstances of imprisonment and chains Paul, has not allowed himself to be chained to fear or anxiety (Phil. 1:7). There is confidence, calm, and cheerfulness in Paul's writing to the Philippians. He continues to pray for the Philip-pians with joy (Phil. 1:4). He has watched God advance the gospel through his own adversity in Rome (Phil. 1:12–18). He remains hopeful about his own release through their prayers and the help of the Spirit of Jesus Christ (Phil. 1:19). He is confident the good work God started in them will be brought to completion (Phil. 1:6). He is pressing forward in his walk with God despite the pressure of his confining circumstances (Phil. 3:12–14). He lives each day in the expectation Jesus Christ could come back at any moment to change him and his circumstances (Phil. 3:21). And his soul is fortified by the thought God is able to supply his every need according to His riches in Christ Jesus (Phil. 4:19).

Paul was a man who clearly practiced what he preached. As Paul invites the Philippians to pursue God's peace he models it as a prisoner in Rome. Here was a man at peace within his circumstances, because here was a man who knew peace with God (Rom. 5:1), enjoyed the peace of God (Phil. 4:6–7), and kept company with the God of peace (Phil. 4:9). Paul enjoyed a divine and sublime peace that was upward, inward, and outward in its dimensions. Through faith in Christ he rejoiced in the Lord always and worried about nothing. Therefore, he encourages the Philippians to take cover in peace from God through prayer that will guard their hearts from undue worry.

During the dark and depressing days of the Blitz in London when German bombers and V1 rockets rained death on the British people, a church bulletin board reminded Londoners "Knees don't knock when you are kneeling on them." The point of that wartime slogan outside that church was to remind people when life conspires to bring you to your knees you are in the perfect position to pray for God's peace and protection. Lives kneeling in prayer are lives that rise fortified by a God-given calm and courage.

That Second World War poster is an echo of Philippians 4:6–7 were Paul reminds the Philippians no man or woman need surrender to fear if they will but yield their fears to God in prayer. Let's follow along as Paul prohibits panic, promotes prayer, and promises peace.

PAUL PROHIBITS PANIC

In writing to the Philippians, the apostle Paul says, "Be anxious for nothing . . ." (Phil. 4:6). This is an imperative in the Greek, a command to desist from anxiety. They were to stop worrying. That's pretty clear, wouldn't you agree? There is little wiggle room here; anxiety is absolutely forbidden for the Christian. The follower of Jesus Christ is not to be a worrywart as taught by Christ (Matt. 6:25, 34). The Bible is unequivocal; anxiety is unbecoming of a Christian under any circumstances.

To understand and appreciate the force of this command, we would do well to appreciate the actual circumstances of the Philippians. As David Jeremiah writes, "Because of their status as citizens of a Roman colony, the Philippian Christians were certainly candidates for anxiety. The persecution from Nero was beginning to boil, and the effects were starting to be felt over the Roman domain. These young Christians knew they would soon be tested in their walk with God."[1] The church at Philippi constituted a big bullseye for the Roman authorities, a target for soft and hard harassment.

You might be thinking anyone who issues a complete ban on worry is not living in the real world, but as we have just established, Paul wrote this command as a Roman prisoner, to a church facing Roman persecution (Phil. 1:7, 13, 28–29). Regardless of our life context, you and I can no more worry as Christians than we can blaspheme God's name, disobey our parents, steal, covet, or commit adultery. In Christian circles worry can often be seen as a respectable sin, but no sin is respectable, and worry is sin for it breaks a clear command of Scripture from the mouth of Christ and the pen of Paul.

Because worry is categorically forbidden, we would serve ourselves well by defining what it is? The word Paul uses for "anxious" is the Greek word *merimnao*, which means "to be torn, or pulled in different directions." Like a man being drawn and quartered, worry pulls the mind apart leaving it divided and distracted. When speaking of anxiety, Paul had in view a divided mind that results in a chronic condition of spiritual instability and ineffectiveness. The apostle James pictures the anxious mind and the doubting heart as a "wave of the sea driven and tossed by the wind" (James 1:6–8). Like a heaving sea, worry produces a life marked by insecurity and instability. To see this syndrome, you need look no further than Martha who is shown in Luke's gospel to be worried to a point of distraction and desperation (Luke 10:40–42).

The worrier trusts God and then doesn't trust God. Within the anxious heart and mind a game of mental Ping-Pong is played between faith and fear. The anxious mind bats things back and forth and cannot decide what to do and who to believe. The anxious mind looks momentarily to God for peace, but then is dragged away to focus on a pressing problem to the point of mental exhaustion and spiritual paralysis.

From this description and definition, we see worry at its heart is a lack of sustained confidence and trust in God's love, wisdom, sovereignty, and power (Isa. 26:3). In teaching His own disciples about the need to stop worrying Jesus clearly identifies worry as "little faith" or a lack of trust in God (Matt. 6:30). According to Jesus, it is especially a lack of trust in God's fatherly character, care, and concern (Matt. 6:31–32). The point Jesus is making is it is unbelievably wrong for a Christian to worry or be anxious when God is our Father and as such knows what we need (Matt. 6:31–34), has compassion for our situation (Psa. 103:13), and is unswervingly committed to meeting us at the point of our need with a perfect gift from above (James 1:17). Therefore, Christians are not to act like nervous orphans who have no father to care for them; they are by contrast to live as the adopted sons and daughters of God secure in the abiding and abundant love of their Heavenly Father (Rom. 8:15–17; 31–39).

Michael Green makes the point when he notes, "A child does not worry all day long whether his house will be there when he gets home from school or whether his parents will have a meal ready for him that evening. Children do not worry about such things because they trust their parents. In the same way, we as Christians should trust our heavenly Father to supply what is best."[2]

How true and how wonderful to meet each new day secure in the love of God our Heavenly Father. Children don't worry, parents worry, but we have a parent in God for whom nothing is a worry, and that is why we can be anxious for nothing.

In returning to Paul's prohibition, it must be said by way of clarification that Paul is not promoting a carefree approach to life. This verse can never to be used to justify an attitude of irresponsibility. To be clear, here Paul is forbidding unhealthy worry not healthy concern. It is interesting to note that earlier in the letter Paul uses the same Greek word used here to describe anxiety to describe Timothy's genuine concern for the Philippians spiritual welfare (Phil. 2:20). Similarly, Paul employs the same Greek word to describe the pastoral concern he bears daily for the all the churches (2 Cor. 11:28). Clearly, there is a distinction to be made between undue anxiety and due concern.

Listen! Not to worry is not the same as not to care. Mothers are not to stop being concerned about their children's welfare, pastors are not to stop being concerned about eternal souls, architects are not to stop being concerned about their calculations being right, politicians are not to stop being concerned about the health of the nation, and soldiers are not to stop being concerned about battlefield dangers.

Some years ago, while pastoring Emmanuel Baptist Church in Toledo, Ohio, I preached a message on the sin of worry from this very passage in Philippians 4:6–7. Within the message I sought to make the distinction between reasonable concern and unreasonable worry, and afterward I received a thoughtful email from a young mother in the church where she shared her struggle to keep "her good worries from going bad." In the email she shared of her ongoing struggle to know the difference and to know when she crossed the line between good and bad worries.

That is indeed a real issue and not an easy one to solve. The line between good and bad worries is a thin one and not an easy one to draw. But perhaps remembering what worry is at its core helps us know when we have crossed the line between legitimate and illegitimate concern. If worry is a divided mind leading to fear and a paralysis of the will, you and I will have a good idea our concerns are moving in the wrong direction when they become debilitating. When our concern is healthy in nature we will be able to manage it by God's grace rather than be managed by it. When our concern is healthy, we will still be able to function as we live by faith in God. It was Dr. Martin Lloyd Jones the great English expositor who I believe said, "Faith is a refusal to panic."

PAUL PROMOTES PRAYER

Paul not only prohibits panic, he promotes prayer. The great apostle encourages the Philippians to pray their worries away. He writes, "Be anxious for nothing, but in everything by prayer and supplication, with thanksgiving, let your requests be made known to God . . ." (Phil. 4:6).

Paul offers them and us a simple antidote to worrying about everything; instead the Christian is to be anxious for nothing, prayerful about everything, and thankful for anything.

According to Paul, the Philippians must not allow worry to pull them in all sorts of directions to the point of desperation and distraction, rather, life's problems and pressures must be allowed to push them in one direction, namely the throne of grace (Heb. 4:14–16). The Christian is not to carry their cares in their own strength and wisdom but to cast their cares on Christ who is able to keep them from falling (1 Peter 5:7; Jude 20–25). The Christian need not worry at any time because they can be "praying always with all prayer" (Eph. 6:18).

The word translated "but" or "instead" is a what is called a transitional adversative. The adversative in the Greek language usually signals a principle that appears in sharp contrast to the one just mentioned, as we see here in Philippians 4:6, "Be anxious for nothing, *but* [transitional adversative] in everything by prayer . . ." Notice the sharp contrast? When facing mounting challenges or during times when life presses in, rather than worrying about those things, the Christian according to Paul is to bring them to the Lord in prayer. Worry holds on to anxious thoughts and allows them to divide the mind and trouble the heart. Prayer, however, releases those anxious thoughts to God and invites the soul to be carefree in the care of God. As the theologian Sinclair Ferguson notes, "Anxiety cannot continue to breathe easily in an atmosphere suffused by prayer."[3] The Bible is clear; worry chokes faith, but prayer suffocates anxiety (Matt. 13:22; Phil. 4:6–7).

I like to think of worry and prayer as oil and water, light and darkness, truth and error, opposites. And like opposites they don't mix. The one is exclusive to the other. The absence of the one is because of the presence of the other. Consequently, people who worry too much tend to be people who pray too little. That is why in times when we are tempted to worry, the Bible urges us to unburden our hearts through prayer (Psa. 27:7–9, 34:5–6; 73:28). Prayer is the means of grace by which we bring our cares and worries to the Lord, and the avenue by which He brings His peace to us. The beginning of believing prayer is the end of unbelieving worry.

That said, our practice of prayer leading to peace will entail several elements. According to Paul in Philippians 4:6–7, our seeking of God's peace ought to be marked by asking (prayer), passion (supplication), specificity (requests), and a remembrance of God's past faithfulness (thanksgiving). In the face of approaching anxiety we must come to God every time in desperate dependence, thankful and encouraged by former answers to prayer, to ask for God's ample help. Prayer is the window through which we escape our fears and the door through which we enter enjoyment of God's peace (Psa. 46:10).

Simply put, prayer brings us before God, and when a man finds himself caught up in the presence of the Most High God, waiting and worshipping, like the psalmist in Psalm 91 notes, his worries melt, his fears crumble, his problems shrink, and his faith grows. Taking cover in God's presence through prayer, the psalmist does not fear the terrors of the night, the dangers of the day, or the disasters that strike at noon (Psa. 91:4–6). As this psalm shows, worry cannot abide within the man who abides in the secret place of the Most High God (Psa. 91:1–2). In the presence of a sovereign God who rules over all, the peace of God begins to rule in the heart of the child of God (Col. 3:15). Blinded by God's glory, grace, and greatness we no longer see our worries as big or our enemies as strong (Psa. 27:1).

In the light of that, it is so important in our praying we focus on the character of God and not our problems. Like Isaiah, we need to see God on His throne, high and lifted up (Isa. 6:1). Notice in Philippians 4:6, the direction of prayer is Godward, Paul tells us to make our requests made known to God. While our worries drive us to God in prayer, it is the glory and greatness of God keeping us in prayer. We are to pray to God who, like the peace He promises, surpasses our understanding, God who can answer our concerns in ways beyond our imagination (Phil. 4:7; Eph. 3:20–21). That being the case, our problem in prayer is we often start our prayers in the wrong place.

In his book *This is Living*, Leonard Griffith eloquently makes this point. He writes:

Too often we start to pray at the wrong place. Prayer should begin not with ourselves but with God—a conscious awareness that we stand before Him as creatures before the Creator, subjects before the King, servants before the Master, children before the Heavenly Father. A university student burdened by a personal problem spent an hour with Phillips Brooks, the great Boston preacher. When he returned to the college, a friend asked him, "What did Dr. Brooks say about your problem?" The student looked surprised. "I forgot to mention it," he said. "It didn't seem to matter anyway when I talked with Phillips Brooks." That should be the effect of prayer, and it will be the effect if we come consciously into the presence of God. Before ever becoming a recital of our own problems, prayer is a devotional exercise whereby we lose ourselves in God and rise from our mortality to his eternity, our smallness to his greatness, our weakness to his power.[4]

That is a good word! Real prayer certainly involves us talking to God about our problems, but the more we talk to God, the more we think about God, and the more we think about God, the less we think about our problems, because the thought of God's love, wisdom, power, sovereignty, and grace overshadows them. Here is a wonderful thought. As we pray and become ravished by God's power and presence, our worries are all gobbled up.

I believe it was Corrie-ten-Boom who famously and rightly shouted from a moving train as it left the platform to a group of embarrassed English ministers, "Don't wrestle just nestle." As you and I abide or nestle under the shadow of the Most High God, His peace begins to fall on our parched and troubled souls like gentle refreshing rain ending drought. Let's nestle not wrestle.

PAUL PROMISES PEACE

As Paul continues he tells the Philippians prayer to God results in peace from God (Phil. 4:7). The conjunction "and" points to the fact peace comes as a consequence of prayerfully seeking God. As sure as day follows night and Tuesday follows Monday, the peace of God follows proper and passionate prayer. It is a package deal; prayer and peace belong together, the one with the other.

Interestingly, for Paul, peace was not the absence of problems but the presence of God in the midst of problems. By implication, the peace of God is not said to bring about a change in their circumstances but a change within them within their circumstances. The peace of God promises to guard their hearts and minds amid the threats. Interestingly, also, Paul doesn't tell the Philippians to seek peace, but he does tell them to seek the God of peace (Phil. 4:6–7, 9). You see no one ever finds peace by seeking peace, peace biblically speaking is the byproduct of seeking God in prayer. When a man finds his way into God's presence through prayer peace will find him.

As we just noted, the peace Paul promises is peace that guards the mind and heart through Christ Jesus (Phil. 4:7). The word "guard" was a military term meaning, "to keep watch over." This was a well-chosen word, for the city of Philippi was a Roman colony and as such was guarded by a company of Roman legionnaires. As the Philippians went about their daily business they were often confronted with the sight of a Roman legionnaire standing guard over the city. Paul is therefore using this word creatively to convey to the Philippians that just as the city of Philippi was guarded round the clock, so the praying church and Christians are under the protective custody of the peace of God. The peace of God through prayer is a peace able to guard the heart of the child of God from the onslaught of worry, the attacks of Satan, and the incursion of sinful desires.

What a wonderful thing to know the Christian is not a sitting duck for the onslaught of fear or worry, but we have available to us the protective shield of God's peace (Num. 6:24–26). We can stand in this evil day and not fall victim to fear (Eph. 6:10–18).

In digging a little deeper we can see this peace is both divine and sublime in nature.

First, it is divine in nature in that it is sourced in God. As "the peace of God," it is necessarily a peace given to us from God (Phil. 4:7). It is by inference and by reference the peace that exists in God as the God of peace (Phil. 4:9; Rom. 15:33). That is amazing! The peace that marks the halls of heaven, the tranquility that surrounds the throne of God, the peace that shapes the character of God, and the peace Jesus showed throughout his life and when facing death is promised to us and can be experienced by us. The Lord Jesus said, "My peace I give to you" (John 14:27).

As a footnote to this, it is important to make a distinction between peace with God (Rom. 5:1) and the peace of God (Phil. 4:7). The first is external and fixed and speaks of our justification before God through faith alone in Christ and His death on our behalf. The second is internal, is subsequent to salvation, is subject to change, and speaks of our confidence in God through prayer and the seeking of God's face. We can never lose peace with God, but we can lose the peace of God. Faith in Christ brings us into an unalterable relationship with God, but the experience and enjoyment of that relationship will greatly depend on the depth of our prayer and worship.

Second, the peace of God is sublime in nature in that it defies human logic and transcends earthly analysis (Phil. 4:7). It is like God's ways and love; it is past finding out (Rom. 11:33; Eph. 3:19). As J. H. Pickford in his commentary on Philippians notes, "All the yardsticks of philosophy cannot measure it; all the analysis of psychology cannot explain it, and nothing else in the world can achieve it. God's peace is boundless in its application to human needs. We cannot explain it; we cannot exhaust it, and God forbid that we exchange it for the false, fleeting peace of the world which is empty and void."[5]

When this divine and sublime peace is experienced by God's people, it produces an otherworldly calm, and when witnessed by the world in the life of a troubled saint, it produces breathless wonder. When Paul speaks of the peace of God as something incomprehensible, he is not implying it is unreal or intangible. No, what Paul means is what is known to us and experienced by us is incomprehensible to a watching world. This is peace no pill can supply, this is peace no doctor can prescribe, this is a peace money cannot buy and death cannot steal.

Think of Daniel and how, when faced with the threat of being thrown into the lion's den for disobeying the king's decree, he composed himself and prayed to God with thanksgiving just like Paul admonishes the Philippians (Dan. 6:1–10). As a result of his loyalty to God, he was thrown into a den of lions at the king's decree, but the irony of the story is while Daniel was able to spend a night in perfect peace, the king who gave the orders spent the night unable to sleep (Dan. 6:16–23). The king was in his bedroom unable to sleep though guarded by soldiers; Daniel was in the den of lions able to sleep because he was guarded by the peace of God that passes all understanding. In learning of Daniel's serenity and survival, King Darius pays homage to the God of Daniel, the One who delivers and rescues (Dan. 6:25–28). You have got to love that. Here we have in the story of Daniel a living breathing example of the promise of Philippians 4:6–7

In adding to the story of Daniel we would do well to recall the death of the English Reformer, John Rogers. In his book *The Five English Reformers* J. C. Ryle tells the account of Rogers fiery death under the reign of "Bloody Mary," Queen of England. Rogers was the first leading Protestant in England to break the ice and cross the river of death as a martyr. This faithful London minister was burned at the stake at Smithfield on February 4, 1555. On the way to his death, he passed by his wife and ten children being allowed only a fleeting glance in their direction. It is also reported he walked calmly and courageously to the stake repeating Psalm 51 for comfort. Up until that moment, men could not tell how English Reformers would behave in the face of death. As to John Rogers behavior in the face of death, the French Ambassador Noallies, who was present to witness the martyrdom, wrote home that Rogers went to his death "as if he was walking to His wedding."[6] Wow!

The prophet Daniel and the English Reformer John Rogers both took cover in a divine and sublime peace that comes to the praying soul. Each of these men withstood the onslaught of worry because their hearts were garrisoned by a sense of God's presence and peace found through believing prayer. Both these men teach us the life that trusts in God and kneels in prayer is able to rise in peace. May their example teach us not to worry but to pray to the God of peace who never worries and who is willing to grant us the gift of His peace through faith in His Son.

No Christ, no peace!

Know Christ, know peace!

CHAPTER 2

KEEPING YOUR BALANCE
TAKING COVER IN A LIFE GUARDED
BY GOD-CENTERED WORSHIP

*God is to me the Great Unknown. I believe in
Him, but I can't find Him.*

Adoniram Judson

I like the movies I watch to have a good ending. I like movies where the
good guys win, and the bad guys lose, where justice is served, where
evil is punished, where good deeds long forgotten are rewarded, where
the right boy gets the right girl, and where the sun rises to announce the
beginning of a better world. I guess I like movies like that for the same
reason I assume you do, they provide us with a temporary escape from
a world where justice is not always served, where the nice guy doesn't
always get the girl, where the bad guys get away with murder, and where
truth is on the scaffold and evil is on the throne.

Let's be honest, life in the real world doesn't feel as good as a feel-
good Hollywood movie. In the real world, cheaters pass exams, terrorists

become folk heroes, sexual deviants become cultural icons, corporate crime gets whitewashed in a bankruptcy court, children are abused, crime bosses live into their nineties and die peacefully in their sleep, and Christians are martyred for their faith. Life in the real world isn't fair. Life seems to be, as someone put it, a theatre in which all the worst people have the best seats. Does it not feel like ours is a world where it is good to be bad and bad to be good? Morally it's all upside down and back to front, the wicked prosper, and righteous suffer.

This, however, is not a new or modern problem. "Why do the righteous suffer?" is an age-old question. It is a question as old as the hills. It is a question that has troubled the best men, men such as Job (Job 21:7), David (Psa. 37:7), Jeremiah (Jer. 12:1), Habakkuk (Hab. 1:2), and Asaph (Psa. 73:2–3). There is nothing new under the sun.

Picking up on that last reference I want to turn our attention to the complaint of Asaph in Psalm 73 regarding the prosperity of the wicked. As Asaph looked out his front window, he was confronted with a world where the blessing and the cursing pronounced in the book of Deuteronomy were reversed (Deut. 28). In his day it seemed like the righteous were being cursed and the wicked blessed. In his world the wicked lived in ease, while righteous lives were marked by hardship (Psa. 73:3–12; 13–14).

To add some color to this man's struggle, let me paint in a little of the background. The superscription tells us the author is Asaph. He was a Levite and was appointed choir director in God's house under the reigns of David and Solomon (1 Chron. 15:15–17; 16:4–7). By implication he was a man of deep piety, a man devoted to God and his neighbor. But as the story goes in Psalm 73, this worship leader almost stopped singing, life spun him around and he became spiritually disoriented. He says, "my feet had almost stumbled" (Psa. 73:2–3). What he was singing didn't square with what he was seeing! His service in God's house didn't connect with the world from which he had come. Because in that world, God doesn't seem to be sovereign. In that world, there's no justice, in that world the wicked prosper, and the righteous suffer. Asaph experienced a crisis of faith. If God is good, then why in the world does it seem good to be bad? As noted, Psalm 73 portrays a man, who according to his own words, almost plunged to his spiritual death because of the seeming prosperity of the unrighteous.

At this point let me say that I'm so thankful for the honesty of this Psalm. When we approach God's Word, we discover God doesn't white-wash the struggles of His people. The saints of God are not airbrushed to perfection on the pages of Scripture. Instead, each is portrayed in both the good and the bad. Bible characters are shown to have hearts of iron and feet of clay. The best men are shown to be, but men at best.

Back when Oliver Cromwell, the protector of England, was having his portrait painted he turned to the man commissioned to do his paint-ing, and said, "Paint me warts and all." In the Bible, God offers a picture of the human experience, warts and all. You cannot read the Psalms and find people who have never been riddled with doubt, or fallen into despair, or been held in the grip of fear, or sinned wildly. No, what you meet in the Psalms is flesh-and-blood characters who struggle and sin just like you and me. That's why Athanasius, the great church leader of the early centuries of church history said:

> Elsewhere in the Bible, you read only that the law com-mands this, or that to be done, you listen to the Prophets to learn about the Savior's coming, or you turn to the his-torical books to learn of the doings of kings, and holy men; but in the Psalter, besides all these things, you learn about yourself. You find depicted in it all the movements of your soul, all its changes, all its ups and downs, all its failures and recoveries.[1]

Psalm 73 introduces us to a believer who failed and recovered, stum-bled and regained his footing, and wrote to tell us about that experience of moving from fear to faith, despair to hope. And through this song, we will discover how to take cover in a life rooted in God-centered worship.

ASAPH'S REFLECTION

The psalm begins with a reflection upon the goodness of God. Asaph begins with a statement of faith. The creedal premise of this psalm is God is good (Psa. 73:1). The Israelite believed God was intrinsically good by nature, good through His many works, and able in His sovereignty to work good out of evil (Psa. 119:68; Gen. 50:20). In fact, the theme of God's goodness acts as bookends to this Psalm. The word "good" forms an inclusio within the poem (Psa. 73:1, 28). God is good, and it is good to draw near to God. Asaph believed that and wants others to believe.

That said the reality is, as the rest of this psalm shows, our belief in the goodness of God will be tested. There are events and experiences within life that will make a dent in that belief. The loss of a child, famine, war, poverty, the seeming silence of God in the face of suffering, and [in the case of Asaph] the arrogance of the wicked. But the psalmist wants us to know that regardless of what we feel, or what we see, God is good, and we must believe that.

Asaph in writing this piece does not deny it is a struggle at times to believe in the goodness of God, but we walk by faith not by sight (2 Cor. 5:7). We must go on holding to the belief that God is good, does good, and brings good out of the bad. Asaph purposely begins with a conclusion (vv. 1, 28), because his faith in God has weathered the storm of doubt, God can be trusted, and he writes to pass that wisdom on to his readers.

This is truth formed on the anvil of affliction. This is costly wisdom for which Asaph paid a price. This man's faith in God's goodness did not come easily, it had to be fought for, and it was hard won. This man's belief in the goodness of God rings true because of the struggle he described and the victory he achieved. It has been well-said, "a faith that has not been tested cannot be trusted." Here is a man whose faith in God's goodness was tested and proven true.

Throughout her book, *A Lifetime of Wisdom*, Joni Eareckson Tada passes along to her readers what she calls "rubies hard won." Rubies of wisdom from a woman bound to a wheelchair for more than forty years,

rubies dug from the ashes of defeat, rubies forged in the furnace of affliction, rubies bought at the price of pain and polished on the grindstone
of hardship. Godly and uplifting insights on living worth their weight in
gold (Prov. 3:13–15).[2]

Asaph's faith in the goodness of God is a "ruby hard won," and we
would do well to listen and learn.

ASPAH'S REMONSTRATION

Following Asaph's reflection, you have Asaph's remonstration. This sweet
psalmist of Israel is singing in a low key as he lodges a complaint with
heaven. His faith is struggling, his feet are slipping, and he is losing his
will to worship. He declares, "But as for me, my feet had almost stumbled; my steps had nearly slipped. For I was envious of the boastful, when
I saw the prosperity of the wicked" (Psa. 73:2–3). Life on the ground
presented this glaring and galling contradiction of the ungodly enjoying
peace and prosperity, what amounts to God's shalom.

What the psalmist believed and what he had been taught in God's
House about the blessing of obedience and what he confronted in life
seemed to be in conflict. The inequity and injustice of it all created for
him a crisis of faith. There was a seeming disconnect between his theology and his experience. The truth that God blesses those who obey Him
didn't square with life on the street. After all, the wicked seem to be free
from the troubles of life and the terrors of death (vv. 4–5); they wear their
violence and arrogance like a necklace (v. 6); they get what they want all
the time (v. 7); they blaspheme against heaven itself and live as though
God does not exist (vv. 8–9, 11); and they enjoy the approval and adula-
tion of an indulgent culture, a society at large that drinks in all the
scandalous and solicitous details of their lives (v. 10). Unlike the righteous, the lives of the wicked and the lawless are marked by peace,
prosperity, and popularity.

As you can imagine this is all getting to Asaph, getting under Asaph's
skin, and irritating his soul no end. It was painful to watch (Psa. 73:16).
How can this be? Why does God allow this to happen? What is the profit

to being godly? This last question perplexed and vexed Asaph greatly
(Psa. 73:13–14).

As Charles Haddon Spurgeon observes,

> *Poor Asaph! He questions the value of holiness when its*
> *wages are paid in the coin of affliction. There are crowns for*
> *the reprobate and crosses for the elect. Strange that the saints*
> *should sigh, and the sinners sing.*[3]

That's exactly where our writer is as he looks out across the world
where reprobates wear crowns, the elect wear crosses, where sinners sing,
and saints sigh. His struggle is shared by many of God's saints throughout history. It's our struggle. It's the struggle of the Christian woman
who won't compromise her standards sexually and who desires God's
design for marriage. Yet she struggles with prolonged singleness, with
increasing loneliness, and with watching girl after girl sleep around, get
married, have children, and live in a nice home.

This is the struggle of the Christian business owner. I was talking to
one recently who plays by the rules yet finds himself undercut in his bids
for business by those who hire illegal workers, and who make deals under
the table to skirt tax laws. It's hard to compete in that kind of environment, the kind of environment that rewards those who don't play by
the rules.

This too is the struggle of the law enforcement officer who has to
stand by and witness criminals circumvent the law with the help of fancy
lawyers or watch cases collapse because witnesses were bullied out of
speaking in court. How galling to watch criminals and violent men leave
the courtroom with mocking grins on their faces. During my time in the
RUC in Northern Ireland, I witnessed this over and over again, and it
made by blood boil and my stomach churn. All testimony to the fact too
often truth is on the scaffold and wrong is on the throne.

This also is the struggle of Christian actors or artists who refuse to
play a certain part in a movie or play because of their moral conviction
and as a result find themselves blacklisted in the world of entertainment.

Finally, this is the struggle of the persecuted saint in the Islamic world or other parts of the world, whose life is under threat, while their tormentors live in ease, protected by a corrupt regime. They feel like lambs being led to the slaughter.

Asaph's woes are our woes, Asaph's world is our world. We can understand his struggle to keep spiritual balance in a world tilted toward the prosperity of the wicked. Sanctification and holiness don't come without a fight. To continue to believe in God, at times, doesn't come easily.

Asaph wasn't the first and he wouldn't be the last saint of God to search for God in the darkness, to feel they're losing their grip on God. Another of God's struggling and searching saints was Adoniram Judson, one of the early Baptist missionaries in Burma.

In his book *10 Who Changed the World*, Danny Akin tells us that during his ministry in Burma, Judson lost his beautiful wife Ann, who was his soul mate and faithful helper. He was just beginning to gain his footing when he faced sorrow upon sorrow in the loss of his little daughter, Maria, to deathly illness. Consequently, he fell into despair and a deep depression. He fled into the jungle and lived there for a while like a hermit, questioning himself, questioning God, and wrestling with his calling and faith.

He demanded all his letters to America be destroyed, he renounced the degree bestowed on him by Brown University. Not stopping there, he gave all his private wealth away, a sizable sum, to missions, and on top of that requested a cut in his salary. Shortly after, he dug a grave near his home, and sat by it for days, just staring into it. On October 24, 1829, on the third anniversary of his wife's death, he said, "God is to me the Great Unknown. I believe in Him, but I do not find Him."

The good news is God's love and power did not fail him or forsake him. Judson emerged from the cloud cover with his faith in God and God's goodness intact. He said of those days, "There is a love that never fails. If I had not felt certain that every additional trial was ordered by infinite love and mercy, I could not have survived my accumulated sufferings."[4]

Our faith may bend, but it need not break.

ASAPH'S RESTRAINT

Yet amid his remonstration, the psalmist exercises godly restraint. Let me explain. The verb in verse two "stumbled" is found in Psalm 62:3 and is used to describe a tottering fence. Applied here we see, spiritually speaking, the psalmist is tottering on the edge of unbelief. His faith in God is being exhausted, and he is thinking out loud within himself as to whether it is worth following God at all (Psa. 73:13–14). He wonders, "What is the good of being good?"

At this point we must assume it would have been tempting for Asaph to go public with his thoughts and questions, but admirably he decides to keep his conflict between him and the Lord (Psa. 73:15). He reasons at the time that to turn his soul inside out in public would have been an abdication of leadership on his part and would prove unprofitable for God's people. What was there to be gained in upsetting the faith of others. Plus, the problem of evil was perplexing enough for him without it being dumped in the lap of young and immature believers (Psa. 73:16, 15). As an esteemed leader he understood his opinion carried weight, and therefore, to go public about his doubts could adversely affect the faith of others. Out of wisdom and love for the congregation of the righteous, Asaph censors himself.

There's an old preacher's story about a blind man who carried a lighted lantern at night and everybody asked him why in the world he carried a lighted lantern when he couldn't see? After all, it was evidently no benefit to him. In answering the questions asked by others the blind man replied, "I carry the lighted lantern, so that nobody falls over me."

That is a good perspective. It's Asaph's perspective. When you or I am in the middle of something painful and hard to understand, that is the very time to show restraint in questioning our faith or expressing our doubts. It's not the time to go public, it's the time to give God the benefit of the doubt, it's the time to cover our mouth with our hand like Job, and it's the time to be careful about what we are going to say and be wise about to whom we are going to say it.

By way of further application, we would do well to be cautious about this increasing call for authenticity in the church today, which calls for people to share their feelings without the balance of spiritual restraint. If we're not careful, this call for authenticity can become dangerous as leaders, and people with problems, get up and spill their guts with no theological boundaries to govern the experience. Often, such unrestrained transparency hurts people, undermines faith, dishonors God, grieves the Spirit, and becomes a playground for the enemy of our souls. Asaph's restraint concerning his own struggle is a cautionary tale to us all, especially those in leadership, to be discerning about the public confession of personal sins and struggles.

Please note, Asaph will eventually share his struggle through the writing of this Psalm, but it will come after his victory over the struggle, it will come at a later date. Asaph understood there is a time and place for everything under the sun, a time to speak and a time to be silent, and he chose the time to speak about his struggle wisely (Eccles. 3:1, 7). He didn't just blurt it out as he felt it necessary, there was no wallowing in public about this crisis of faith. As we noted earlier, detailing his struggle comes later and is couched and bookended in affirmations of faith in the goodness of God (Psa. 73:1, 28). He writes later and in a manner that is honest but profitable to his readers. Asaph is happy to talk about the struggle to believe, but it is beautifully balanced with a testimony to the fact that despite the struggle God's people nevertheless have faith that overcomes the world (1 John 5:4).

ASAPH'S RECOVERY

The good news is, although Asaph stumbled and nearly fell over into unbelief, he did regain his balance and kept walking by faith and not by sight. According to the text, the road to recovery began with a visit to the sanctuary, God's house (Psa. 73:16–17). The worship of God, high and lifted up, caused a paradigm shift in Asaph's thinking. He came to see things differently, he was not on the losing side but on the winning side. While there in God's house, praying, singing, and meditating on Scripture, a transformation took place; Asaph's pain gives way to peace, and Asaph's vexation gives way to relaxation. This visit to the sanctuary of God changes his mood, reorients his heart, focuses his mind, and shifts his perspective. To paraphrase what Warren Wiersbe notes about Asaph, "The turning point comes when he stops being a philosopher, and starts being a worshipper."[5] Change comes when he stops asking questions and starts offering worship.

There is a pivotal shift of focus going on in the text and something we must not overlook. The dominant pronouns within the psalm tell the story. In the first part of the psalm, the dominant pronoun is "they" (Psa. 73:3–12). Asaph is focused on the wicked. In the middle part of the Psalm, the dominant pronoun is "I" (Psa. 73:13–17). Asaph is focused on himself in comparison with the wicked. In the latter part of the psalm, the dominant pronoun is "you" (Psa. 73:18–22). Asaph is focused on God, not himself, and not the wicked.

As I stated a couple paragraphs ago, the turning point comes when Asaph stops being a philosopher and starts being a worshipper. Up until this point, Asaph's thinking was without theological reflection. He sought to understand life under the sun without consulting the God who resides above the sun, the God who made and governs all living creatures beneath the sun (Psa. 115:3; 47:2–3). Up until this point he was leaning on his own understanding, and that was a mistake (Prov. 3:5–6). Asaph's problem was he became fixated with the wicked and himself and took his eyes off the Lord. Thankfully, worship acted as a corrective lens to help him see the world from heaven's perspective. In worship before God, Asaph was reminded that God is sovereign, judgment is coming against the wicked, and glory awaits the righteous (Psa. 73:17–20, 24–26).

I think by now we can safely deduce from this shift in focus the importance of private and public worship as a protection against the onslaught of doubt and unworthy thoughts about God. As Asaph learned to his benefit, the secret to spiritual sanity is gazing long and hard upon

God while only glancing at our problems. As one of my former pastors used to say back in Northern Ireland, "The outlook maybe gloomy but the uplook is glorious." Life does take on a different complexion when we look into the face of God (Psa. 34:5).

I love the fact Isaiah saw the Lord in the year King Uzziah died and it made a difference (Isa. 6:1). I love the fact the apostle John saw a throne in heaven amid the panorama of the last days and it made a difference (Rev. 4:1–2). By implication, life will never look right without us first seeing the Lord, and seeing Him behind our todays and over our tomorrows (Psa. 16:8). Listen! Worship is so critical in our search for security because it moves God from the circumference to the center and delivers us from the distortion of self-absorption and the fears of the present.

Digging deeper into this section of the psalm, we see private and public worship offers the worshipper two things, new horizons and new hope.

Worship Offers New Horizons

It is clear from Asaph's encounter with God, worship in the sanctuary put an eternal spin on what he was looking at and lamenting over (Psa. 73:17–20). Before the throne of heaven and within God's glorious presence, Asaph came to see things differently. From on top of the holy hill of godly worship, the psalmist is given a whole new perspective on things (Psa. 24:3–4). Sitting quietly within the sanctuary meditating upon God's eternal person and plans, a new panorama unfolds before Asaph, a prophetic panorama that turns the world the upright (Psa. 46:10).

Through worship Asaph comes to see the wicked are like passengers on the Titanic, totally oblivious to the danger ahead. Unbeknown to them, they are on a collision course with the submerged iceberg of God's coming judgment. Their dreamlike lives will soon become a nightmare. When God awakes in wrath the lives of the wicked with pass like a bad dream. This is the raw and red-blooded reality behind the imagery of these verses and others (Psa. 73:18–20; 37:1–2, 7–11).

Asaph has been looking through the wrong end of the telescope; he has been earthbound, time-locked, and fleshly in his thinking. He allowed his immediate emotions to cloud eternal truths. I like how Ray Galea puts it:

> Asaph had pictured the life of the wicked as a still photograph rather than a motion picture with a tragic ending. He had seen their present success but forgotten about their future failure.[6]

Worship before a holy, sovereign, faithful, and eternal God reminded Asaph of what he forgot. In the end God wins, in the end the righteous triumph, and in the end the wicked lose out. You see worship makes God big, makes man small, and makes the future near. Worship is like a telescope; it is not something you look at but something you look through, so it was through God-centered worship Asaph was brought to see the tragic end of the wicked (Prov. 14:12). When it comes to the wicked there is nothing there to envy or be jealous about, in the end pity perhaps, but not envy. When God awakens in judgment you will not want to be them.

Bottom line, when it comes to our struggle with the prosperity of the wicked we need to begin with the end. We need to filter our thinking and reactions, through an eternal perspective (2 Cor. 4:16–18). We need, as C. S. Lewis once said, "to follow a thing to its bloody conclusion." The broad, populated, and easy road, as Jesus points out, is the one that leads to destruction (Matt. 7:13–14).

Rembrandt's painting "The Night Watch" is on public show in the Rijksmuseum in Amsterdam, or most of it is. The powers that be in the art world once reduced its size, removing three people from the original. What a way to treat a masterpiece. Cropping it made it a different picture.[7] In making a comparison, we see Asaph in his crisis of faith crop and narrow his spiritual vision of the world. In doing so he lost perspective and was left with a vision of the world missing crucial elements. But through worship Asaph's spiritual vision was restored, and a complete picture of the world and God's governance of it was restored. Worship afforded him a new horizon.

Worship Offers New Hope

With his eyes wide open, Asaph sees the world differently, but he also sees what a fool he has been in God's presence (Psa. 73:21–22). He has acted like a dumb animal before the almighty. Metaphorically speaking, he acted like a bull in a china shop with his grumbling and murmuring. He went as far as to question God's justice and doubt the benefits of faith in God. He soon saw himself as a disgrace to grace.

But, the silver lining in the whole thing is that while he was losing his grip on God, God did not lose His hold on him (Psa. 73:23–28). The "nevertheless" of verse 23 points to the fact there could have been an altogether different outcome to this struggle apart from God's loving-kindness and forgiveness. God did not abandon him but continued to guard and guide him (v. 23); God went so far as to promise him future grace in heaven (v. 24–25), and God never stopped pouring His strength into Asaph (v. 26).

As Asaph worships God in His house, he encounters a God who does not reward him according to his sins (Psa. 103:10), a God who remains faithful in the face of his faithlessness (2 Tim. 2:13), a God whose mercies to him are new every morning (Lam. 3:23–25). In worship, Asaph receives not only new horizons but new hope. Asaph found and so can we that "there is a love that never fails."

In the face of man's injustice to man, Christians must fill their hearts and minds with the thought of God's graciousness to us and the pledge of His love throughout eternity. It is by standing at the foot of the cross and reflecting on God's love and justice in Christ that we prevent our feet from slipping. In a world of insecurity, we find our security in God's love for us (Rom. 8:31–39).

In closing, we see Asaph regained his balance because God was holding his hand (Psa. 73:23). As he was falling, God was holding him up. As David says in Psalm 37, "Though he [the good man] falls, he shall

not be utterly cast down; for the Lord upholds him with his hand"
(Psa. 37:23–24).

When I think of that verse I have vivid memories of walking in the
park with each of my three girls when they were young and just getting
on their feet. As we walked with their hand in mine, I could feel them
fall as their little legs gave way under them. But they never fell far, for at
that moment when I felt the tug of their hand as they collapsed, I would
simply swing them back unto their feet, and off we would go again stroll-
ing through the park. This happened more than once while out walking,
but I just whipped them back unto their feet each time.

Psalm 73 is the story of a man of God who lost his footing because
of the prosperity of the wicked and injustice in the world. Though he
slipped, he didn't fall far, for God whipped him back unto His feet
through a worship experience in God's house that afforded him new
horizons and new hope. Psalm 73 is a declaration that it is good to draw
near to God in worship, for God is good, does good, and will work all
things together for good. Asaph was assured that a good God will ensure
good triumphs over the bad, and faith in Him pays.

Asaph takes cover in that reality and so should we.

CHAPTER 3

DON'T BE SURPRISED
TAKING COVER IN A LIFE GUARDED BY A PROPER VIEW OF SUFFERING

*We must not spread our sails of profession in a
calm, and furl them up when the wind riseth.*

William Gurnall

The story is told of two brothers who got into a fight with each other. Hearing the commotion from a distance, the father of the boys rushes to break up the scuffle and find out what is going on. After scolding both of them, he asked who started it, who struck the first blow? The younger of the two answered, "Dad, I hit him back before he hit me." Now there is a young man who is not going to allow himself to be surprised. He anticipated what was coming and prepared himself for it. Either drawing from intuition or past experience, he was ready.

In a similar manner Christians need to anticipate persecution and suffering at the hands of an unbelieving world. The Bible does not allow the follower of Jesus Christ to expect to get to heaven without some scrapes and scars. Peter says to the pilgrims of the Dispersion, "Beloved, do not think it strange concerning the fiery trial which is to try you, as though some strange thing happened to you; but rejoice to the extent that you partake in Christ's sufferings . . ." (1 Peter 4:12–13). Paul says to the Philippians, "For to you it has been granted on behalf of Christ, not only to believe on Him, but also to suffer for His sake" (Phil. 1:29). Jesus taught in the Sermon on the Mount, "Blessed are you when they revile you and persecute you and say all kinds of evil against you falsely for my sake" (Matt. 5:11). In Doctor Luke's record of the early church in the book of Acts we are told, "We must through many tribulations enter the kingdom of God" (Acts 14:22).

Salvation by grace is not a free pass on suffering. Wounds of all kinds—physical, personal, psychological, and political—await those who love and follow the crucified Savior. The history of the church is a trail of blood and as such teaches us persecution is the normal rite of passage in the Christian life. We must not forget that one of the great symbols of Christian commitment is the cross. Jesus told his followers to take up their cross and follow him (Matt. 16:24–25). The cross was an instrument of death, a symbol of sacrifice, and one that suggests blood and killing. Jesus is therefore teaching us to be a card-carrying Christian involves carrying a cross and a willingness to shed our blood and face death for Him. The Christian must not be surprised at suffering. As God's lambs among the wolves, we can expect to be hunted, hounded, and harassed (Luke 10:3). As some unknown author said so well, "History has shown that God's people have been persecuted sometimes by Pharaoh on the throne, Haman in the government, and Judas in the church."

Today, Christians all around the world continue to be led like lambs to the slaughter (Rom. 8:36). Whether we are talking about the Middle East, Africa, or Asia, Christians are being beheaded, buried alive, displaced, crucified, sold into slavery, and having their property confiscated. In parts of the Middle East, the Christian community has been decimated to a fraction of its former numbers because of ISIS and other forms of Islamic terror.

The reality is, today the persecution of Christians is one of the largest human rights issue of our generation. In his excellent, edifying, and eye-opening book, *Christians in the Crosshairs*, Gregory C. Cochran writes,

> *According to a study recently released by the Pew Research Center, about three-fourths of the population of the world lives under a government that has highly restricted religious freedoms. Of those restrictions, the majority are aimed at Christians. Some international humanitarian agencies have estimated that 80% of all religious persecution in the world today is aimed at Christians.*"[1]

Now, while the church in America has largely been shielded from this persecution because of providence and constitutional protections, for which we are deeply thankful, times are changing. Today in the United States, militant secularists, humanists, and atheists, people who like to ignore the First Amendment and twist the meaning of separation of church and state, are increasingly involved in seeking to drive Christians from government posts, educational chairs, and army chaplaincies. The Christian who preaches the exclusivity of the gospel of Jesus Christ is labeled a bigot; the Christian who opposes gay marriage is called homophobic; the Christian who questions the transgender agenda is called hateful; the Christian who espouses the biblical record of Creation is pegged as anti-intellectual; and the Christian who questions the growth of governmental power is considered antisocial. The list goes on, but the point is simple. Winds of social and ethical change are blowing across America, and they are blowing into the faces of Bible believing Christians.

Yet as I have hinted and highlighted already, none of this should surprise us. The Master's Minority has always faced the brunt of the world's hatred and hostility. Jesus reminds us in John's Gospel they hated Him, and they will hate anyone who looks like Him and lives for Him (John 15:18–19). The world is no friend to those who are <u>in</u> it, but not of it (John 17:15–18). That is why I want to argue in this chapter that God's people need to take cover in a realistic view of the Christian life and a proper view of suffering.

To help us take cover in a proper view of suffering I want us to study the apostle Peter's words in 1 Peter 4:12–19. In this passage we will see suffering is not a strange thing for the Christian, it ought to be expected (v. 12), even rejoiced in (v. 13), and certainly considered in the light of the coming glory to be ours in heaven (v. 13).

By the way, in these words, Peter is fulfilling Jesus's words in Luke 22:32 when he was told to strengthen the church following his own fall and restoration with regard to his unwillingness to suffer for Christ. Peter was now willing to suffer for Christ, and he writes this letter asking others to join him. He writes around AD 64–65 from Rome to encourage God's people to take their stand for Christ (1 Peter 5:12–13).

PETER ENCOURAGES REALISM

Historically, Peter writes this letter when the early church was on the doorstep of a 200-year period of blistering persecution triggered by mad Nero's burning of Christians in Rome. Writing to Christians in four major provinces of Asia Minor, the great apostle calls on them to view this gathering storm with some theological realism (1 Peter 1:1, 4:12–19). He doesn't promise them their best life now, and he doesn't call them to think positive thoughts, rather he reminds them their theology informs them that suffering is to be expected and is the same kind of suffering Jesus endured. Biblical realism confronts them with the fact God's people are no strangers to suffering.

Persecution Is Inevitable

The believers of the Dispersion were not to think of their suffering as a strange thing (1 Peter 4:12). Just as soldiers expect death, athletes expect pain, students expect homework, and mothers expect exhaustion, so

Christians should expect the world's hostility and hatred. In fact, according to Peter earlier in the letter, suffering is what we are called to by God (1 Peter 2:21). Christians who don't think they should suffer are not thinking.

On one front we should expect to suffer because Jesus was hated and as we follow Him, and He reproduces His life in us we can expect to face the same experience (John 15:18–19). He is our example in this (1 Peter 2:21–23). I hope you know the less the world knows about Jesus the more they like Him, but the more they know about Jesus as revealed in Scripture the less they like Him. The Jesus most people believe in is a Jesus of their own imagination, a Jesus who tolerates sin, loves everybody, and doesn't send anybody to hell. So, you and I can anticipate the more we remind them of the real Jesus the less they will like us.

On another front we should expect suffering because the light of Christ in us will expose the darkness around us and make people uneasy (John 3:19–21; Eph. 5:8–14). Think about this, men without conscience hate those who stir the conscience. Holiness and Christlikeness on the part of the church will unsettle and agitate a godless society. Just being what Christ has called us to be is enough to get us into trouble with the world (1 Peter 4:12–14). Persecution is the inevitable response of a world in which men love darkness rather than light.

Expectations are important for they tend to shape our behavior and control our conduct. That is why it is critically important our expectations about life and especially the Christian life be true and not false. Wrong expectations lead to disillusionment and disappointment, while right expectations breed hope and stability. Peter understands this and therefore prepares the believers in Asia Minor to embrace suffering not as something strange but something they are to receive with rejoicing. 1 Peter helps the church get real about life expectations. Not all marriages are heaven on earth (1 Peter 3:1–6). Coming to Christ doesn't end our struggle with sin (1 Peter 2:11). Obedience and faith doesn't lead to a pain-free life (1 Peter 1:6–7; 2:19). Our best life is not now but later and therefore we must be patient under suffering (1 Peter 2:20; 4:12–13; 5:10–11).

The actress Helen Hayes once told a story about cooking her first Thanksgiving turkey. She readily admitted she wasn't much of a cook, but after several years of marriage and dodging the tradition of cooking a turkey at Thanksgiving, she plucked up the courage to give it a try. Realizing the danger of disappointment, she sat her husband and son down before the meal and said, "This may not come out exactly the way you want it to. If it's not a good turkey, don't say a thing. Without any comment, just stand up from the table, and we'll go to the nearest restaurant and eat." Shortly after, Helen walked into the room with the turkey. Her husband and son were already standing with their coats and hats on![2]

As this story illustrates, expectations do shape behavior and control conduct. We tend to conduct our lives and daily affairs based on a set of assumptions. In relation to trouble and trails, 1 Peter 4:12–19 must shape our expectations and frame our understanding.

Having said all that, it is worth underscoring a qualification Peter makes in the text related to suffering. While suffering for righteousness sake is inevitable, Peter warns about unnecessary suffering, the kind of suffering brought on by our own faults and foolishness. In verses 15 and 16 Peter says, "But let none of you suffer as a murderer, a thief, an evildoer, or as a busybody in other people matters. Yet if anyone suffers as a Christian, let him not be ashamed, but let him glorify God in this manner" (1 Peter 4:15–16). The suffering God blesses is the suffering due to our Christian witness not the suffering brought about by our sinful behavior. Let us be mindful as followers of Christ not to draw fire from the world for no good reason. May it be the gospel offends people, not you or me being offensive (Gal. 5:11). Let us suffer as Christians not cretins.

Persecution Is Intentional

While Peter alerts us to the fact persecution is inevitable, he also wants us to understand it has God-appointed purposes. Scripture tells us when persecution happens, when we suffer for being a Christian, it is not happenstance, for it takes place according to the will of God (1 Peter 4:12,

19). God appoints affliction, and God privileges us with suffering (1 Thess. 3:3; Phil. 1:29). Why? Well in the immediate context we see God intended the fiery ordeal of Christian suffering within the Roman Empire to try and test them (1 Peter 4:12). Harkening back to his earlier comments on faith being "tested by fire" the apostle Peter eludes to the fact God sovereignly and strategically uses trials to test the Christian's spiritual mettle (1 Peter 1:6, 4:12). Just as fire tests, refines, and purifies silver and gold, so suffering providentially permitted and rightly handled, purifies, and strengthens Christians (Prov. 27:21; Job 23:10). The readers were to be encouraged in seeing God's good purposes within their difficulty. Trials were permitted by God's good hand for the purpose of approving and improving their faith, not disapproving it. Their fiery ordeal at the hands of the Romans was at the same time God's refining fire (Mal. 3:1–3).

Before entering the ministry, I worked as an engineer for an aerospace company in Belfast called Short Brothers. Our plant nudged up against the shoreline of Belfast Lough and bordered the large shipbuilding company Harland and Wolf, where the Titanic was built.

Once in a while during lunchtime sitting with my friends, we could catch a glimpse of the latest super tanker getting ready to head out to the open sea before being handed off to Shell Oil Company or British Petroleum. When completed, each ship headed out of Belfast Lough into the rolling Irish Sea to be put through its paces. These maneuvers were known as sea trials.

On the open sea the ship's engines and equipment are tested to ensure all systems are working and ready to perform their intended purpose. As you can imagine the sea trial was designed not to disprove the ship but to approve the ship. The purpose was positive not negative.

God does the same in the life of the church and the Christian when He allows fiery trials to come our way. His desire is not to disprove our faith, but to prove it (Rom. 5:3–5; James 1:2–4). His purpose is not to destroy us but to develop us, to bring us to a new level of purity, commitment, and trust in Him. As the great English Baptist preacher C. H. Spurgeon reminds us, "The anvil, the fire, and the hammer are the making of us."[3] That is why we should be hesitant to sidestep a trial for we may well be avoiding a blessing. That is why we need to turn a deaf ear to the peddlers of a health and wealth gospel who tell us faith exempts us from trouble, when 1 Peter teaches us trouble strengthens and grows faith.

If we were to go outside the context of 1 Peter 4:12–19, we would see God has many designs for persecution in the life of His people. In Acts 8:4 we see God used persecution to forcefully spread the gospel. In Philippians 1:12 we see God use Paul's imprisonment to advance the gospel. In Acts 9 with Paul and Acts 16 with the Philippian jailer, God used the suffering of his servants to bring people to faith in Christ. In 2 Corinthians 1:8–9 we see God use trouble to cultivate reliance upon Him. In Philippians 1:14 we see God use Paul's imprisonment to challenge and embolden the faith of other saints. In James 1:12 we see God use pressure to increase the believer's eternal rewards. And in Hebrews 12:7–8 we see God use chastening to separate the true believer from the false believer.

God does not pain his children for nothing; there is purpose in the pain, and there is design in the difficulty. Given that reality we should never waste our sorrows or doubt the wisdom and love of God in the middle of the test. While in the middle of a muddle or a puddle is not the time to doubt God's goodness, God is up to something bigger than our relief. As the North African bishop Augustine argued, God uses hardship and trials to build Christian character and commitment. He writes:

> For, in the same fire, gold gleams and straw smokes; under the same flail the stalk is crushed, and the grain threshed; the lees are not mistaken for oil because they have issued from the same press. So, too, the tide of trouble will test, purify and improve the good, but beat, crush, and wash away the wicked. So it is that, under the weight of the same affliction, the wicked deny and blaspheme God, and the good pray to Him and praise Him. The difference is not what people suffer but the way they suffer. The same shaking that makes fetid water stink makes perfume issue a more pleasant odor."[4]

PETER ENCOURAGES REJOICING

As Peter writes to comfort and challenge the saints of the Dispersion, he not only encourages realism, he also encourages rejoicing. In the face of suffering they are not to be surprised or sullen. He says, "but rejoice to the extent that you partake of Christ's sufferings, that when His glory is revealed, you may also be glad with exceeding joy. If you are reproached for the name of Christ, blessed are you, for the Spirit of glory and of God rests upon you" (1 Peter 4:13–14).

The striking thing about this part of the instruction is, although suffering is the norm for the Christian, the Christian's response is anything but normal. To embrace losses and crosses in a spirit of rejoicing is not natural; it is supernatural. It is joy produced by the Holy Spirit (1 Thess. 1:6). It is joy from faith that counts on the grace of God (James 1:2–4). It is joy that treasures Christ above all (Acts 5:41). It is one thing to endure a trial; it is quite another thing to exult in it, and only God can produce that.

Let us be clear, Peter is not calling the trial joyful, but he is saying the fruit and benefits of the trail can be a source of great joy. The suffering itself is bad, but the spiritual outcomes of the suffering can prove to be a source of deep spiritual satisfaction. Peter tells them to rejoice because, one, it is a privilege; two, it opens the door to greater joy in the life to come; and three, because those who suffer for Christ's sake meet God in a special way in the midst of the pain.

Let's unpack those three thoughts.

The Privilege

Suffering as a Christian makes us a partner in the kind of suffering Christ experienced and endured (1 Peter 4:13). Jesus was a man of sorrows, despised, oppressed, afflicted, and rejected by men (Isa. 53:3, 7). When the Christian is bullied, when the church is bloodied, at that moment they get to identify with Christ in His unjust treatment at the hands of the world and Peter says that is a privilege. In the crucible of soft or hard persecution, it is our joy to fellowship with Christ in His sufferings (Phil. 3:10). While it cuts against the grain of the soft evangelicalism of today, this text is saying suffering for the gospel allows the Christian to look like and live like the Lord Jesus Christ, and that is a blessing. The early disciples were found, "rejoicing that they were counted worthy to suffer for His name" (Acts 5:41). Paul even describes suffering as a gift granted to us by God (Phil. 1:29).

At this point it would be good to remind ourselves the call to suffer was a redemptive reality Peter had to grow into. Initially Peter wanted a cross-less Christianity, a faith in which Jesus didn't have to die, and crosses didn't have to be carried (Matt. 16:21–26). However, the events of Jesus's arrest, trial, death, burial, and resurrection changed all that, and now Peter gladly embraces the thought of suffering for Jesus's sake. In fact, Peter's life ended in martyrdom and crucifixion (John 21:18–19). Church tradition records he was martyred under Nero, crucified upside down because he did not feel worthy to be crucified like his Lord.

Please notice in all this, Jesus suffering for us does not exempt us from suffering. We must not confuse vicarious atonement where Jesus dies for our sin with vicarious suffering. We mustn't think that because Jesus suffered for us, we don't have to suffer. The truth is Jesus's suffering on the cross for us doesn't mean life is going to be pain-free. Jesus's atoning death means we do not have to die for our sin, it does not mean we do not have to die to self, die for others, or die for Christ (Phil. 2:1–11). We cannot and we must not preach or practice a Christianity in which Christ does all the dying. To follow a crucified Savior and Lord inevitably leads to our suffering because as they hated Him they will hate us (John 15:18; 1 Peter 2:21–23).

Although, there is a wonderful compensating truth we need to add to the mix. According to the writer, to the Hebrews Jesus's own suffering qualified Him to be an aid and help to His people when they are tempted and troubled (Heb. 2:18; 4:14–16). That means as we share in His suffering He shares His sympathy and grace with us while we live and die for Him. He understands what we are going through, and He undertakes for His people in the midst of their pain (John 16:33). He has known the stigma of illegitimacy, the pangs of hunger, the cold shoulder of rejection, the drag of weariness, the wound of betrayal, the horror of suffering, and the terror of death.

Amy Carmichael was a young girl from my native Belfast in Northern Ireland who gave her life to God and to world evangelism. In giving her life to missions she also gave her heart to India for fifty years, establishing the now-famous Dohnavur Fellowship. Her focus was on rescuing young girls from forced prostitution in the local Hindu Temples. Later in life Amy suffered a terrible fall that confined her to her bed for the rest of her days. She never returned to Northern Ireland. It is reported that from her bed she continued to minister to many through prayer, counseling, and witnessing. Above her bed it is said she had two plaques. One said, "Fear Not," while the other said, "I Know."

Like all God's true servants, Amy Carmichael survived her suffering understanding Jesus knew all about her struggles. It was her privilege to suffer for Him and her privilege to know His love and support in the midst of the suffering.

The Prospect

Continuing to instruct and inspire his readers, the apostle Peter reminds them suffering leads to glory (1 Peter 4:13). In anticipating the Lord Jesus's return in power and majesty at His Second Coming, "when His glory is revealed," Peter tells the saints of the Dispersion they will be exceedingly glad at that future moment to have been partakers of Christ's suffering. The enduring of present pain is gloriously offset by the anticipation of future unending joy (1 Peter 1:6–9; James 1:12).

It is worth noting how Peter shows several times in this epistle how in Jesus's own life sorrow was followed by joy, mockery was followed by honor, and suffering was followed by glory (1 Peter 1:11, 21). Following His humiliation, you have Jesus' exaltation (Phil. 2:5–11; Heb. 1:3). And this pattern of suffering followed by glory holds true for God's people. Throughout this letter Peter holds this carrot in front of the bloodied noses of God's suffering saints as an incentive to persevere (1 Peter

1:3–6; 5:1–4; 5:5–6; 5:10–11). The "now" of present suffering must be processed with the "then" of coming glory in view. Peter wants all Christians to know our suffering is but "for a little while" and will soon give way to "pleasures forevermore" (1 Peter 1:6; Psa. 16:11). Peter's companion, Paul says, "For I consider that the sufferings of this present time are not worthy to be compared with the glory which shall be revealed in us" (Rom. 8:18).

The point is inescapable. The church militant on earth must keep an eternal perspective on her present circumstances and conflicts. This is not our best life now. We must look beyond our temporary troubles to the hills of glory, to life everlasting, to Jesus on the throne, to a time without time when there will be no more crying, sighing, or dying (Rev. 21:1–4).

The British pastor Tim Chester in his excellent book "The Ordinary Hero" helps us better grasp this point and apply it. He writes:

> Our life is but a moment, a breath. It's the tick of a clock. A blink of an eye. A click of the fingers.
>
> You get one life, one chance. And there's no replay, no rewind.
>
> Don't live for the moment. Live for eternity.
>
> Your suffering and shame are for a moment. Your reward is forever.
>
> The area in which you live now is for a moment. The location where you will spend eternity is forever.
>
> Your temptations and your sin are for a moment. Hell is forever.
>
> Your pride and achievements are for a moment. God's glory is forever.
>
> Your career is for a moment. God's "Well done good and faithful servant" is forever.
>
> Your love life and your sex life are for a moment. Your union with Christ is forever.

Your home now is for a moment. Your home in your heavenly Father's house is forever.

Your money and possessions are for a moment. Your heavenly treasure is forever.

Your pension is for a moment. Your heavenly inheritance is forever.

John Hooper, a Protestant during the reign of Mary Tudor, was facing martyrdom. He was urged by a friend to renounce the faith. "Life is sweet, death is bitter," his friend told him. Hooper replied: "Eternal life is more sweet, eternal death more bitter."

Reflect for a moment. Think of the trials you are undergoing. Think of the price you pay to serve Jesus. Think of the price you refuse to pay to serve Jesus. Think of the risks you take. Or don't take. Imagine looking back on this after a million, billion years of eternal glory.[5]

Enough said.

The Presence

As if the promise of future glory were not enough, Peter goes on to add the guarantee of present blessing. The apostle writes, "If you are reproached for the name of Christ blessed are you, for the Spirit of Christ and of God rests upon you" (1 Peter 4:14). Embedded within this section of the letter is the promised presence of God through the indwelling Holy Spirit. To be cursed by men for the sake of our gospel testimony is to be blessed by God. It is at these low points of pressure and persecution we come to enjoy a heightened awareness of God's presence and peace within. The self-same Spirit who rested upon Christ throughout His life and ministry rests upon the follower of Christ (Isa. 11:2; Matt. 3:16). The Spirit is the Divine Comforter who comes alongside us to strengthen us in the battle (John 14:26; 16:7–8).

The testimony of Scripture is whenever we suffer for Christ and His cause, the Lord becomes nearer and dearer to us. You see that principle and pattern at work in the lives of Daniel's three friends when thrown into the fiery furnace (Dan. 3:24–25), you see it at work in the stoning of Stephen (Acts 7:56), and you see it at work in the final trial of Paul (2 Tim. 4:17). As I said earlier, it is at our lowest moments we enjoy a heightened awareness of God's presence and peace.

Corrie ten Boom, who was transported to Ravensbruck concentration camp along with her sister Betsie for the crime of hiding Jews, is testimony to this fact. Enduring squalid conditions, living under the constant threat of death, and ultimately losing her father and sister to the Nazi death camp, she nevertheless persevered by faith in Christ. In fact, the day before her sister Betsie died, Betsie pulled Corrie close to her as she lay dying in a dirty hospital ward and whispered in Corrie's ear: "We must tell them that there is no pit so deep that He is not deeper still. They will listen to us, Corrie, because we have been here."[6]

After her sister's death and her own release due to a clerical error, Corrie did take that message to the world, and the world did listen. The people of God in the worst conditions have lived to enjoy the benediction of God's peace, presence, provision, providence, and power in and on their lives. There is no pit so deep Jesus is not deeper still. When the enemy gives us no rest, the Spirit of glory and of God rests upon us.

Samuel Rutherford the seventeenth-century Scottish Presbyterian who was banished to Aberdeen for daring to challenge the absolute right of kings famously said of his prison experience, "Jesus came into my prison cell last night, and ever stone flashed like a ruby." Again, when the enemy gives us no rest the Spirit of glory and of God rests upon his people.

PETER ENCOURAGES RELIANCE

As Peter pulls the curtains on this section of his letter and changes the subject to pastoral leadership, he concludes with a word of exhortation. Given their growing jeopardy, Peter encourages his readers to place their lives into God's keeping. He says, "Therefore let those who suffer according to the will of God commit their souls to Him in doing good, as to a faithful Creator" (1 Peter 4:19). Their sense of vulnerability was answered in God's ability to protect and preserve the souls of His people.

The word "commit" is a banking term and carries the idea depositing a valuable item or a sum of money for safe keeping. Peter's point then is just as people deposit their valuables in banks, so the believer puts their trust in God. They trust their yesterdays with all their untidiness, they trust their todays will all their challenges, and they trust their tomorrows with all their possibilities into the safe keeping of a Sovereign and loving God. This is what David did while facing adversity (Psa. 31:5), this is what the Lord Jesus did while hanging on the cross (1 Peter 2:23), this is what Paul did while imprisoned and facing death (2 Tim. 1:12), and this is what we all must do. Our insecurities melt before the blazing truth of God's power, faithfulness, and ability to keep and protect His people. Nothing troubles God and nothing need trouble those who trust Him, because true trust in God leads to perfect peace (Isa. 26:3; 12:2).

In the midst of the unknown, with signs of a gathering storm of persecution ahead under Nero, Peter instructs his readers to focus on what they know to be true about God. God is a faithful creator, He is more dependable than the rising of the sun, His mercies are new every morning, and great is His faithfulness (Lam. 3:22–25; 2 Tim. 2:13). While the saints of the Dispersion could not know what the future held, they could enter the future holding to the truth of God's genuineness and faithfulness (Mal. 3:6; James 1:17). In their losses and crosses they must not allow themselves to suffer a loss of confidence in God (Psa. 27:1–3, 13–14). They must keep on keeping on, secure in the knowledge they are kept by God (Psa. 121:4; Jude 24). Christians must bank on the faithfulness of God!

On one occasion a church leader in Melbourne, Australia, introduced the well-known missionary James Hudson Taylor to a congregation as "our illustrious guest." No one including the Presbyterian moderator who introduced him was ready for the first sentence of Taylor's response: "Dear friends, I am the little servant of an illustrious

Master." Despite his many years and effective ministry in China, Hudson Taylor never saw himself as a spiritual giant but as a weak man who was able to do great things for God because he could count on God being with him. His was a life of unwavering faith in the faithfulness of God. Writing about missions and ministry he once said: "Want of trust is at the root of almost all our sins and all our weaknesses, and how shall we escape it but by looking to Him and observing His faithfulness." He continued: "The man who holds God's faithfulness will not be fool-hardy or reckless, but he will be ready for every emergency."[7]

Faith in the faithfulness of God does indeed make us ready for every emergency. In a world of shifting tides and gathering storms, it is a wonderful thing to anchor one's hope to the faithfulness of God, an everlasting faithfulness (Psa. 119:90), fixed (Psa. 89:2), unfailing (Psa. 89:33), infinite (Psa. 36:5), great (Lam. 3:23), and incomparable (Psa. 89:8).

Hatred of Christians is inevitable. Don't be surprised. The world hates us, because it first hated Jesus. To align our lives with Christ will invariably put us at odds with the culture and make us a target for a Christ-rejecting world. But when we do come under fire, we must and we can take cover in the knowledge we suffer according to the will of God, that God has allowed this test to refine our faith, it is something we can rejoice in, suffering is followed by glory, God's benediction will rest on us, and God can be trusted with our todays and tomorrows.

CHAPTER 4

THE REAL ENEMY
TAKING COVER IN A LIFE GUARDED BY A KNOWLEDGE OF THE ENEMY

I believe Satan to exist for two reasons: first,
the Bible says so; and second, I've done
business with him.

D. L. Moody

When World War I broke out, the war ministry in London dissemi-nated a coded message to a far-flung British outpost in the heart of Africa. The message from the homeland when decoded said, "War declared. Arrest all enemy aliens in your district." This prompt reply was received back in London, "Have arrested ten Germans, six Belgians, four Frenchmen, two Italians, three Austrians, and one Amer-ican. Please advise immediately who we are at war with."[1]

It goes without saying when it comes to the pursuit and prosecution of war you need to know who and what you are up against. The enemy must be clearly identified before they can be engaged. No fighting force wants to go blind into battle regarding the strength, weaponry, location, and tactics of the enemy. As far back as six centuries before Christ, the famed Chinese general and military mastermind Sun Tzu was teaching soldiers a simple strategy: know your enemy.

The Christian life is a call to arms and what is true in the field of military conquests is also true in the realm of spiritual warfare, we need to know the enemy. According to the Bible, the Christian fights on three fronts: against the world, the flesh, and the devil. The follower of Jesus Christ faces an internal threat from the flesh that opposes God's work in us through the Holy Spirit (Gal. 5:17), an external threat from the world that pressures us day after day to compromise our Christian convictions (Rom. 12:1–2), and an infernal threat from the devil who goes about seeking to destroy vulnerable believers who let their guard down (1 Peter 5:8). It is vitally important Christians know the danger they are in, the enemy they face, and the spiritual counter measures God has provided in Jesus Christ. This world is not a playground where Christians have fun; rather it is a battleground where Christians fight for their spiritual lives.

In these evil and frightening times, it is critical we take cover in a life guarded by a knowledge of the enemy of our souls, Satan. The devil is the real malevolent and malignant force behind the evil happening in our world. Paul describes Satan as the "god of this world" in his second letter to the Corinthians (2 Cor. 4:4). The apostle John in his first letter tells us "the whole world lies under the sway of the wicked one" (1 John 5:19). Both Paul and John would remind us the real enemy behind our enemies is the devil. Our foe from below is the one who sponsors sin in all its forms across the world. These verses urge us to look behind the visible forces assaulting the people of God and see an invisible figure who relentlessly stokes the fire of animosity against all that is good and godly. Theologically speaking, Satan is the original sinner, and much of the worlds evil originates from him.

When it comes to prostitution, Satan is the real pimp. When it comes to war, he is the real antagonist. When it comes to false religions, he is the real cult leader. When it comes to crime, he is the real thief and murderer. When it comes to totalitarian governments, he is the real dictator. When it comes to persecution, he is the real inquisitor.

Again, the real enemy behind our enemies is the devil. To a large degree, the real enemy is not the people we see opposing the Gospel but the person and powers we don't see "for we do not wrestle not against flesh and blood, but against principalities, against powers, against the rulers of the darkness of this age, against spiritual hosts of wickedness in the heavenly places" (Eph. 6:12).

That is why by the way we need to rethink how we see those who oppose the Gospel and demean Christ. We need to train our sights on the real enemy behind our enemies. We need to go backstage on life and understand there is an invisible war raging between heaven and hell, and earth is the theater of war (Job 1–2). And Paul would remind us for the most part our visible enemies are being used by the invisible enemy. Satan is the puppeteer; they are the puppets. It is Satan who blinds the minds of the Islamist, the cultist, the humanist, the abortionist; it is Satan who takes them captive (2 Cor. 4:4; 2 Tim. 2:26).

Listen to David Roper as he addresses this very point:

> Behind every human power is the power of darkness. Paul says clearly that our struggle is not against human beings, but against the spiritual powers that control them. Men and women who embody evil are not the enemy. They are the victims of the enemy, "taken captive to do his will" (2 Timothy 2:26). It does little good to rail and rage against those whom the devil has cruelly blinded and deceived; we must rather do battle with the devil who has deceived them.
>
> Life is like a Punch and Judy show. When the puppet-villain puts in an appearance, we can tongue-lash him and hurl rocks at him or take him out with a club. But what have we accomplished? The man behind the curtain will simply place another puppet on the stage and begin to pull the strings again. Far better to go behind the scenes and take out the puppeteer.[2]

That is a good word and a timely reminder to ask God for compassion for those who have no compassion for us. Also, to see the war on truth and the fight against evil as more than a political or human conflict. Firstly and fundamentally, it is spiritual in nature and must be fought as such with spiritual weapons (2 Cor. 10:4–5).

Satan is indeed a formidable enemy, an enemy to us, and an enemy to our enemies, and therefore it is incumbent upon us to take cover in knowledge of his ways and weapons and the Gospel countermeasures God has given us to oppose and defeat him. To that end, I want to offer several principles for standing up to Satan in these evil days as outlined by Paul in Ephesians 6:10–18. This passage constitutes a boot camp for spiritual warfare; here we learn how to stand our ground and fight back.

TIME TO SOBER UP

First, Paul teaches us it is time to sober up. In writing to the Ephesians, this apostle of Jesus Christ wants them to be alert and alive to the threat posed by their adversary the devil. Paul wants them to be cognizant of the fact they have a wicked enemy (Eph. 6:16), they live in an evil day (Eph. 6:13), and there is an array of evil forces implacably against them (Eph. 6:11–12). Six times in the space of two verses Paul will use the word "against" to communicate they have a fight on their hands (Eph. 6:11–12). They must be opened-eyed and clear-headed about the fact that as followers of Christ they live in the crosshairs of hell itself. The Devil and his demons oppose the work of God in them and the work of God through them.

Given their background and situation, I am sure this did not come as a surprise to the Ephesians. The book of Acts tells us the city was a nest for satanic activity, as seen in Paul's encounter with the demonic (Acts 19:11–20). Plus, many of the believers came to Christ from the world of black arts (Acts 19:18–19). Few in the church at Ephesus needed to be schooled in the reality of spiritual warfare, but a clear and compelling call to watchfulness is a good thing. Staying vigilant is not an easy thing to do, soldiers get lazy, guards get tired, and nations get complacent and become victims of surprise attacks. The Christian warrior must therefore stay alert to stay alive.

As we have noted, the Ephesians lived behind enemy lines and were targets for spiritual assassination. Like a policeman patrolling the streets of Belfast during the Troubles in Northern Ireland or an American soldier walking the streets of Fallujah during the Iraqi campaign, the Christian in Ephesus needed to be vigilant. This passage speaks directly to the need for spiritual sobriety and moral watchfulness (Eph. 6:18). Watchfulness and prayerfulness are required in the light of an enemy who is always watching us, always watching to see if we will let our guard down, not to take him seriously and therefore make ourselves sitting ducks (Mark 14:38; 1 Peter 5:8).

Each day requires we put ourselves on notice of the danger our infernal enemy poses to our walk with Christ and our work for Christ. He is always looking for that vulnerable moment, that season in life, when he can take a deadly shot at our life in Christ. In Luke 4:13 we see him leave the Lord Jesus after the temptation in the wilderness with the intent of reengaging his battle with Christ at a more opportune time. This shows us Satan works on the principle if at first you don't succeed try, try, again. Luke tells us his departing from Christ was for the sole purpose of reloading. Satan operates just like a terrorist or enemy sniper in that he will lie in wait for the right moment to strike with deadly force. Satan carefully chooses his moment to attack.

Reflecting on that caused me to think about those certain times and seasons when the enemy might chance his luck.

- Number one, during the time of one's conversion just like the Thessalonians (1 Thess. 1:5–6, 3:4–5).
- Number two, during a time of sickness and suffering just like Paul (2 Cor. 12:7–10).
- Number three, during a time of physical exhaustion just like Christ (Matt. 4:1–3).
- Number four, during a time of notable spiritual blessing just like Peter (Matt. 16:13–20, 21–23).

- Number five, during a time of idleness just like David (2 Sam. 11:1–4).
- Number six, during time of spiritual pretense or hypocrisy just like Ananias and Sapphira (Acts 5:1–3).

Look and learn. Satan is not a trigger-happy gangster but a patient sniper. He waits for the best moment to pull the trigger. We must therefore put on the whole armor of God and watch with all prayer. Remember, eternal vigilance is the price of liberty.

Some time ago my father-in-law Gordon told me a story about his days in the Royal Air Force just after World War II. Leaving his native Scotland, he went to England for basic training. Following a full day of training and a grueling run, the squad was marched to a mock grave on the airbase. At the top of the grave was a headstone and on the headstone were the words, "Here lies the neglectful." As you can imagine the whole point of the exercise was to remind these airmen that vigilance and following your training is the price of life and liberty.

That is no less true for the soldier of the Cross and the follower of the Lamb. To neglect prayer, worship, the studying of Scripture, church life in the body of Christ, separation from the world, repentance, the cultivation of humility before God, and walking in the Spirit, is to dig your own spiritual grave. To mix my metaphors, as a sheep in God's fold don't make yourself a sitting duck for the enemy.

TIME TO SQUARE UP

Second, Paul teaches us it is time to square up. The soldier is not to be a solitary figure. He marches in columns, he fights in platoons, and he belongs to regiments. Old warriors will tell you on the one hand they fought for God and country, but on the other hand they really fought for the man next to them. There is a camaraderie among soldiers unlike almost anything else in the world. There is love and a bond among these men and women forged in the heart of battle. The soldier knows that united they stand, divided they fall. An army at war with itself, through dissension and division, will never defeat the enemy.

None of this is lost on the apostle Paul as he urges the believers at Ephesus not to surrender their loyalty to Jesus Christ. In speaking of spiritual warfare Paul addresses them as single fighting unit, he addresses them as a band of brothers in verse ten, and he employs the plural "you" throughout this section of the letter. Their stand is to be a united stand. They are to go up against the enemy shoulder to shoulder and side by side. They are to join forces one with the other and come alongside each other under the fluttering banner of "One Lord & One Faith" (Eph. 4:4–6). Within the church every person who is in union with Christ is in union with everyone else in union with Christ. In the face of the enemy, the church must close ranks, look out for each other, and act in unison for the good of all. The Psalmist reminds us it is when the body of Christ as the family of God dwells together in unity, God commands His blessing (Psa. 133).

As just noted, the book of Ephesians headlines the fact that through our reconciliation to God those who are in Christ have been reconciled to one another. There is one body, one faith, and one Father of all (Eph. 4:1–6). The walls dividing us have been torn down through what Christ did on the Cross (Eph. 2:14–18). We have been made one in Christ and have equal access to our Father in heaven (Eph. 2:18). And in the context of spiritual warfare, Christian unity is a powerful weapon (Eph. 6:10–18). Why? Because a redeemed and reconciled Christian community is a glorious reversal of Satan's work of cosmic disruption and disharmony. A harmonious and unified community of Christians signals the triumph of the Gospel and is a harbinger of God's future plan to brings all things in heaven and on earth together under the Lordship of Christ (Eph. 3:10–11; 1:10).

Along this line, the Roman army was known for its courage and discipline. In biblical times, the Roman Army was a fierce and formidable force to be reckoned with. Julius Caesar invaded Britain in 55 BC with only 10,000 men. He beat the Gallic tribes of France at the battle of Alesia three years earlier, despite being out numbered four to one. Everyone in the Roman Empire knew the strength of the Roman Army lay not in its numbers, but its discipline. A united army doesn't need to be a large army to be victorious. While the barbarians tended to rely on numbers and mob tactics, the Roman generals drilled their legionaries to form a disciplined "triple line." If charged by cavalry, they could adopt a "square" formation. If bombarded by a hailstorm of arrows, they could adopt the "tortoise" formation behind an interlocking wall of shields. If the generals and legionnaires saw an opportunity to advance in battle they could reorder the army into a "wedge" formation that galvanized the soldier's strength, allowing them to punch holes in the enemy lines. The Roman army was proof positive that united we stand, divided we fall.[3]

Our spiritual survival and impact as God's people in a world at war with God depends on our ability to close ranks and live in community with each other. This is our version of the Roman Phalanx. Writing to the Colossians Paul said, "For though I am absent in the flesh, yet I am with you in spirit, rejoicing to see your good order and steadfastness of faith in Christ" (Col. 2:5). Interestingly, the phrase "good order" is a military term and speaks of an unbroken and orderly line of soldiers showing a united front. Paul's desire for the believers at Collosse was they would continue to act as a well-organized army showing a united front in the face of the enemy.

May we take this example to heart. May we live out our Christian lives in community with God's people. May we not forsake the assembly of God's people on the Lord's day (Heb. 10:24–25). May we find common cause with other Christians in furthering the Gospel through evangelism (Phil. 1:27–30). May we submit to our leaders and follow their direction (1 Thess. 5:12–13). May we make a contribution to the war effort by bringing our spiritual gifts to bear upon the body life of the church (1 Cor. 12:12–31). May we forgive, pray for, love, and bear one another's burdens (Eph. 4:32, James 5:16; John 13:34–35; Gal. 6:2). May we be so tight with one another we give the devil no room to work among us (Eph. 4:25–33).

In August of 1776, while signing the Declaration of Independence, Benjamin Franklin one of American Founding Fathers famously said, "We must all hang together, or assuredly we shall hang separately." Clearly, he was saying if his fellow American patriots did not band together and remain united in the fight against the British, they would each go to the gallows separately. He knew the enemy is always strategizing to divide and conquer.

Satan is no different, so sober up, and square up.

TIME TO STAND UP

Third, Paul teaches us it is time to stand up. We have already made mention of the fact the believer is up against an array of evil powers and principalities (Eph. 6:12). There is an entire realm of spiritual entities predisposed to hindering and harming us through false doctrine, sexual perversion, political censorship, and solicitation to sin. What is the Christian to do? Well, the Christian is to be strong in God's power by putting on the whole armor of God so we are able to oppose the wicked one who is opposing us. The follower of Jesus Christ is not to stand down in the face of the enemy but to stand up. Three times in this passage the Ephesians are exhorted to resist, stand, and withstand the enemy (Eph. 6:11, 13, 14). Remember, the Devil will retreat and run when we resist him in the power of the Son of God who resisted his every temptation (James 4:7; Matt. 4:1–11)

We are to resist him when he tempts us to doubt God as he did with Job (Job 1–2). We are to resist him when he inflates our pride as he did with Peter (Luke 22:31–34). We are to resist him when he seeks to disrupt our work for God as he did with Paul (1 Thess. 2:18). We are to resist him when he tells us there is a greater good outside the will of God as he did with Eve (Gen. 3:1–8). And we are to resist him when he encourages

us to play church and play the hypocrite as he did with Ananias and
Sapphira (Acts 5:1–11).

One of the ways we can stand up to Satan is by understanding the
schemes and strategies he uses against us. Here in Ephesians 6, Paul
speaks of his "wiles" or schemes (Eph. 6:11). In his second letter to the
Corinthians, Paul communicates the fact that as believers we are not
ignorant of the devil's methods (2 Cor. 2:11). The Bible profiles Satan for
us and shows us his tactics, methods, and allies. God's word provides us
with some great opposition research on the enemy behind our enemies
and how we might better stand against him. Thankfully the Christian
does not fight blind.

Let's take a minute and learn about the enemy.

The Devil's Titles

One of the ways we can better understand what and who we are up
against is to study Satan's names and aliases. In these descriptions we
are given a description of his nature and angle of attack. Here is a sampling of his titles:

- Satan or adversary (Job 1:6–7)
- Devil or slanderer (Eph. 6:11)
- Wicked one (Eph. 6:16)
- Tempter (1 Thess. 3:5)
- Accuser (Rev. 12:10)
- Father of lies (John 8:44)
- Ruler of demons (Matt. 12:24)
- God of this world (2 Cor. 4:4)
- Prince of the power of the air (Eph. 2:2)

Careful reflection on these names will help you grasp the nature
of the beast you are up against, and you will be able to start to pre-
dict and anticipate the ways in which he will oppose you. To be fore-
warned is to be forearmed.

The Devil's Tactics

The Bible in no small measure provides us a dossier on Satan. Open the Scriptures and you will see the devil is mentioned in the opening chapters of Genesis, and he is also mentioned in the closing chapters of Revelation, and between these bookends we are provided all kinds of information on the Satan and his black arts. Here is a sampling of the tactics he uses:

- Illicit sex (1 Cor. 7:5)
- Pride (1 Chron. 21:1–8)
- False doctrine (1 Cor. 11:13–14)
- Guilt (Rev. 12:10)
- Temptation (1 Thess. 3:5)
- Sickness (2 Cor. 12:7)
- Opposition (1 Thess. 2:18)
- Unwitting people (Mark 8:32–33)
- Angry bitterness (Eph. 4:26–27)
- Idle gossip (1 Tim. 5:11–15)
- Harshness (2 Cor. 2:11)
- Unequal unions (2 Cor. 6:14–15)
- Disunity (James 3:13–18)
- Questioning God (Gen. 3:1, 5)
- Fortune telling (Acts 16:16)
- Counterfeit miracles (2 Thess. 2:9–10)

When we study these verses, we are made familiar with the plays the devil runs, it is as if God has given us the playbook of the opposing team before the game. Imagine what it would be like if the coach of Alabama knew what the coach of Auburn was thinking before the big game. Imagine what it would be like if the coach of Ohio State knew what the coach of Michigan was thinking before the big game. It would be an advantage no doubt. Well, the Christian has that very advantage over the opposing team; we know their tactics and that prepares us for victory.

The Devil's Time

Something not to miss in the text is Paul talking about the evil day in which the Ephesians lived (Eph. 6:13; 5:16). This reference to the "evil day" is an acknowledgement on the part of Paul that the Christian lives between the fall and the restoration of all things at the Second Coming of Christ. This is a time when God in His sovereignty has given Satan a long leash, whereby he is permitted to go to and fro throughout the earth seeking whom he may devour. Someday he will be bound for a thousand years at the end of human history and then cast into the lake of fire, but that is still in the future (Rev. 20:1–4, 7–10). Presently, we are in an age marked by evil and the evil one, a day where the moral tide is against us (Gal. 1:4). According to Jesus as with the time of His death, this hour in history is marked by the power of darkness (Luke 22:53).

It is good to be reminded bad things can and will happen to God's people. This is a dangerous time to be a Christian; it is the evil day. Every day is a challenge to our walk with God and is tantamount to a walk through a moral minefield. Let's not forget we are living behind enemy lines. Let's not be looking for our best life now or a golden age of Christianity within history. The kingdom awaits the coming of the King.

Several years ago, my wife and I spent our twenty-fifth wedding anniversary over an extended weekend in San Diego. It was memorable for several reasons. One, we got quality time with each other reminiscing on God's goodness and the love He gave us for each other. Two, I got to preach in the pulpit of Dr. David Jeremiah at Shadow Mountain Community Church, which was a huge blessing. And three, we got an insider look at the Navy Seal Training Facility on Coronado Island through a friend who was an active Navy Seal at the time. That was the day that I learned the motto of the Navy Seals is "The only easy day was yesterday."

Just as with the Navy Seals, so with the spiritual warrior, there are no easy days. This is an evil day requiring us to endure hardship as a good soldier of Jesus Christ and to fight the good fight of faith with courage and commitment (2 Tim. 2:3–4; 1 Tim. 6:12). We must stand tall for Christ.

TIME TO SUIT UP

Fourth, Paul teaches us it is time to suit up. Along with moral vigilance, a pursuit of Christian camaraderie, and standing up to the devil's schemes, the spiritual warrior must next be strong in the Lord and the power of His might (Eph. 6:10). God strengthens His saints by clothing them with power as they put on the whole armor of God (Eph. 6:11, 13). It is by cladding themselves with the provided spiritual armor the Christian is able to withstand the assault of the wicked one and remain victorious in the evil day. Just as God clothed His servant Gideon with spiritual power, He will cloth us (Judges 6:34)

It ought not to be forgotten Paul wrote the letter to the Ephesians during his first imprisonment in Rome where he found himself regularly chained to a Roman soldier (Eph. 6:20; Phil. 1:13). No doubt as Paul stares upon the armor of the Roman legionnaire his imagination is stirred to immediately see an analogy to the Christian life. Just as the Roman legionnaire dare not go into battle without putting on his whole armor, (belt, breastplate, shoes, shield, helmet, sword), so the Christian dare not wade into battle with the world, the flesh, and the devil without God's given protections (Eph. 6:10–20).

In seeking to be clothed with power, it is my conviction that putting on the whole armor of God is a call to the constant embracing of Christ in the Gospel. In Romans 13, Paul tells the believers in Rome to "put on the armor of light" and in almost the same breath tells them to "put on the Lord Jesus Christ, and make no provision for the flesh, to fulfill its lusts" (Rom. 13:12, 14). It would seem within the context of Romans 13 putting on the armor of God is synonymous with living in the good of the Gospel of Christ. Putting on the armor of light, putting on the Lord Jesus Christ involves a remembering of, a rejoicing in, and a relying on who we are and what we have in Christ (Eph. 1:3–14; 4:17–24; 5:8–14).

Dr. Jim Rosscup, my professor at The Master's Seminary who taught Bible exposition faithfully and fruitfully for many years, states this point eloquently when he writes concerning Ephesians 6:10–18:

Every part of the armor is what Christ is and provides to
believers . . . Christ is finally all of the six portrayals of armor.
He is the truth (John 14:6), righteousness both imputed and
imparted (1 Cor. 1:30), peace which He "is," "established,"
and "preached" (Eph. 2:14–17), the perfect example of faith
in God and the grace giver of it through His Word (Eph. 2:8;
Rom. 10:17), wearer of the helmet that consists of salvation
and Savior to those who believe (Isa. 59:16; Matt. 1:21), and
the very Word of God which the Spirit wields as His sword,
making timely use of any aspect in it (John 1:1; 1 John 1;1;
cf. 2 Cor. 13:3).[4]

From this we see again putting on the whole armor of God means putting on Christ. Spiritual safety therefore resides in our abiding in Christ, our treasuring of Christ, our following of Christ, and our praying to Christ (John 15:5; Phil. 3:7–10; Col. 2:6–7; Heb. 4:14–16). As we link our lives to Christ by faith, we unite ourselves to the One who defeated Satan by means of His death and resurrection, and therefore our lives are made strong in the Lord (Eph. 1:19–23). Strong enough to stand in the evil day. Strong enough not to be outsmarted by the devil. Strong enough to put the devil to his heels.

When Satan comes knocking, the wise Christian lets the indwelling Christ answer the door, so when the devil sees the risen and triumphant Christ residing in and presiding over our lives, he tucks tail and runs. He remembers Calvary and scoots. He remembers the open tomb and hides. The good news in the good news of the Gospel is that as we submit to God and resist the devil in the power of God's Son the devil flees from us (James 4:7). With Christ in us we can overcome the world, the flesh, and the devil "because He who is in you is greater than he who is in the world" (1 John 4:4; John 16:33). As we draw close to Christ, the devil begins to keep his distance.

That is why it is imperative as Christians we arm ourselves with the Gospel and that we preach the Gospel to ourselves on a daily basis. As we seek to fulfill Gospel imperatives or commands, we need to increasingly embrace and experience Gospel indicatives or truths. Power for performance in life lies in our rehearsing and living out the benefits of Christ's saving work for us. After all, Paul spends the first three chapters in Ephesians rehearsing who the Christian is and what the Christian has in Christ before there is a call to walk worthy of the Gospel (Eph. 1–3; 4:1). The Gospel is not the ABC of the Christian life but the A–Z of the Christian life. Being strong in the Lord is being strong in Gospel truth, Gospel life, Gospel joy, Gospel peace, and Gospel intentionality.

To come to faith in Christ requires someone to preach the Gospel to us, but to grow in faith and the knowledge of the Lord Jesus Christ requires we must preach the Gospel to ourselves morning, noon, and night. Remember the Gospel proclaims Satan's defeat; therefore, it is in that Gospel we find our victory (Rom. 8:37; 2 Cor. 2:14). A Christian without a good experiential knowledge of the Gospel is a city without walls or an army without ammunition.

In closing this section let me tell a story related to our family name. John De Courcy was a strong, brave, and God-fearing Anglo-Norman knight who arrived in Ireland in 1176 and conquered a considerable amount of land. Along the way, as one might imagine he made his fair share of enemies. One of his enemies Sir Hugh De Lacy conspired to capture and kill him with the help of some insider information gathered from some of De Courcy's own men. De Lacy learned De Courcy basically lived in his armor and was a formidable warrior, but once a year he took his armor off to worship on Good Friday. On that holy day he wore no armor and carried no shield or sword. He walked around the church five times barefoot and then spent the day in church kneeling in prayer.

Information in hand De Lacy decides to spring a trap by sending a group of his men to descend on De Courcy on Good Friday. According to history, De Courcy fought valiantly with a cross pole killing thirteen of De Lacy's men, but with no armor or weapons the great warrior was eventually taken. The enemy found him undefended and without his armor for a brief time and pounced.

The enemy of our souls is no different. He waits and watches to see when our love for Christ grows cold, or our life in Christ becomes routine and then he pounces. We must put on Christ each and every day, we must feverishly love the One who has loved us and is able to make us more than conquerors through His love, through His Gospel.

IT IS TIME TO SPEAK UP

Fifth, Paul teaches us it is time to speak up. Speak up to God in prayer. In Ephesians 6:18, Paul tells the Ephesians to be "praying always with all prayer." They were to put on each piece of armor in prayerful dependence upon God. Paul wants the Ephesians to understand a biblical call to arms in spiritual warfare first begins with the clasping of our hands in prayer. The Christian warrior stands up by kneeling. The Christian army marches on its knees. Paul modeled the importance and influence of prayer to the Ephesians by recording two prayers he made on their behalf (Eph. 1:15–24; 3:14–21). In this practice, Paul was communicating there is power and protection in prayer. Prayer links the Christians weakness to God's strength, prayer is as our forefathers portrayed, the slender nerve that moves the omnipotent arm of God.

Interestingly, the section in Ephesians 6:14–20 comprises one long sentence in the original Greek, and it would seem the call to prayer beginning in verse 18 is the element that ties everything together. The armor of God is to be put on prayerfully. By implication, prayer then is a means of engaging in spiritual warfare. In our wrestling with the devil we first wrestle with God in prayer seeking His wisdom, providential protection and strength. In the letter to the Colossians, Epaphras is said to "labor" or "wrestle" in prayer (Col. 4:12). Prayer is wrestling, prayer is warfare.

Many examples in the Word of God marry this relationship between prayer and spiritual victory. King Jehoshaphat and his people prepared to face their foes through praise and prayer, and God supplied them a great triumph (2 Chron. 20). Daniel and his friends did not turn back in the day of battle because they confronted the threat of death through a night spent in prayer (Dan. 2:17–23). Jesus faced His trials by bathing

His life in prayer (Mark 1:35; Luke 5:16; Heb. 5:7). The apostles James and Peter talk of resisting the devil by means of submitting to God in prayer (James 4:7; 1 Peter 5:6–9). Each of these examples remind us we can do more to secure our spiritual safety after we have prayed, but we cannot do more until we have prayed. As the old saying goes, "The devil trembles when he sees the weakest saint upon his knees."

Have you ever thought about why prayer can be such a struggle? Have you ever thought about why the devil hates prayer? Well, the answer lies in the fact prayer is warfare. The devil knows prayer spells disaster for his kingdom and work, and that is why he will meet us on the very threshold of prayer and give us a hundred reasons to do something else. That is why we must endeavor to pray always with all prayer. Prayer must become a holy habit, a reflex response in the face of crisis, challenge, and conflict. Like the Ephesians we must:

- Pray regularly "praying always"
- Pray variously "with all [kinds] of prayer"
- Pray passionately "and supplication"
- Pray dependently "in the Spirit"
- Pray expectantly "with all perseverance"
- Pray corporately "for all the saints"

May we all get serious about prayer as a means of spiritual protection. May we all heed the admonition and instruction of Christ who taught His own disciples to pray to God the Father that He might deliver them from the evil one (Matt. 6:13). The prayerless Christian is the powerless Christian.

Abraham Lincoln used to tell a humorous story on himself. He spoke of two Quaker ladies who were discussing the relative merits, strengths, and prospects of Abraham Lincoln and Jefferson Davis during the Civil War. One of the ladies said, "I think Jefferson will succeed because he is a praying man." The other lady snapped back, "But so is Lincoln a praying man." The first lady retorted, "Yes, but the Lord will think Lincoln is joking."[5]

Let's pray that when we pray the Lord doesn't think we are joking. Let's pray that when we pray the devil is not laughing. Let's get serious about prayer, let's reboot our prayer life. Because if we don't live our lives on our knees in prayerful dependence upon God, the devil will bring us to our knees in spiritual defeat.

As we close this chapter, safeguard your spiritual well-being by taking cover in a real and true knowledge of your enemy. Understand his nature, study his history and future, learn his ways, but most of all appreciate he is a defeated foe. Stand with others in standing up to him and stand in the power of Christ who routed the forces of darkness by means of His death, burial, and resurrection. Remember we are not fighting for victory but from victory.

CHAPTER 5

THE BEGINNING OF THE END
TAKING COVER IN A LIFE GUARDED BY THE HOPE OF JESUS' GLORIOUS RETURN

Our enemy is preaching an Islamic eschatology,
while the Church is silent about hers.

Joel Rosenberg

Several years ago, during a visit to the Ronald Reagan Library in Simi Valley, California, I was intrigued to learn President Reagan had very poor eyesight. It was so bad that earlier in his life it got in the way of his military service. Understandably, to compensate for this visual deficiency he wore glasses and later contacts. Alongside this I was fascinated to discover he wore a nearsighted lens on his right eye and a farsighted lens on his left eye. Consequently, he would read his speech with his right eye and watch the people's reaction with his left eye. President Reagan was a man who focused on the near and the far.

There is a good lesson to be learned from the practice of President Reagan and his use of both a nearsighted and farsighted lens. In looking upon the world and the emerging events of our day, the Christian must take both a near and far look. We must simultaneously live in the meantime with a view to the end time, and Jesus's soon return. We must look beyond the temporal world; we must look up and away from our present and painful circumstances in the anticipation of a coming kingdom (2 Cor. 4:16–18; Col. 3:1–4). While the immediate news of the day often captures our attention with all its alarm and horror, we must push past the depressing news of what our world is becoming and view in Christian hope what the world will become when the Lord Jesus returns in power and glory to establish a new heaven and new earth (Rev. 19:11–16; 21:1–5). The distant look of His return to earth as King of Kings and Lord of Lords must be allowed to shape and reinterpret how we see the world and the events of our day (2 Peter 3:10–13).

It is easy to become alarmed if we remain nearsighted. After all, the Middle East is burning, Israel is in the crosshairs of her Arab and Muslim neighbors, Iran and North Korea are promising the world a nuclear holocaust, morally the days of Noah and Lot are upon us, famine and natural disasters abound, wars and rumors of wars fill our conversation, economic globalism is on the rise, false religious pluralism is spreading, and the church is increasingly like the world. But all this bad news must in a way be viewed as good news because the signs of our times are pointing to the signs of the end time and the recapture of earth by heaven at the return of Christ. The Bible tells us things will get worse before they get better (2 Tim. 3:1–5, 13). We must not be nearsighted alone, we must also be farsighted. To survive and thrive in a world gone mad, we as Christians must begin with the end, we must constantly and confidently keep an eye on the horizon as we look for the second coming of Christ in the clouds with power and glory (Matt. 24:27–31; Luke 21:25–28; Daniel 7:13). We need a view of the future informed by the Bible not by emotions or immediate human affairs.

At this point it is good to be reminded that thinking prophetically is a very practical and positive thing to do. It is a misnomer to believe seeking those things that are above is harmful to life on earth. The Bible teaches and history attests that those who think most of the next life are those who excel most in this life. There is a sense in which the study of prophecy does for us what travelling into space has done for the scientific world. Scientists have learned much about our world by going outside it in space travel and looking back. They have learned things about the human body, weather patterns, and the location of natural resources on earth to name but a few. Things, which they would never have been learned had they not broken free from an earthbound perspective. In a similar way, the study of Bible prophecy carries us out into the future and gives us a perspective on our world we would otherwise not have. That perspective helps us make better sense of our day and the world we live in. This heavenly mindedness makes us of greater earthly use.

According to the Bible one of the best things you can do for yourself in your present circumstances is to take a good long and hard look into the future. The blessed hope of Christ's appearing helps us better stand, serve, and speak for Christ (Titus 2:13). Here are some of the benefits of studying prophecy:

- It invites the blessing of God (Rev. 1:3).
- It builds confidence in Scripture (2 Peter 1:19).
- It exalts the supremacy of Christ (Rev. 19:10).
- It fosters church commitment (Heb. 10:24–25).
- It fortifies us for spiritual warfare (Rom. 13:11–13).
- It promotes evangelism (Matt. 24:14).
- It advocates holiness of life (1 John 3:3).
- It comforts the bereaved (1 Thess. 4:13–18).
- It engenders endurance in trials (James 5:7–11).
- It promises justice to the persecuted (2 Thess. 1:5–10).
- It establishes the sovereignty of God (Isa. 44:6–8; 46:8–11).

As we pursue maximum security in a world forever reeling between danger and disaster, we need to urgently take cover in a life guarded by the wonderful hope of our Lord's glorious return. In the last days, men's hearts will fail them for fear as they see terrifying events unfolding across the world, but the followers of Jesus Christ need not fear or allow their hearts to become troubled for they have His promise to cure and secure them (Luke 21:26–28; Mark 13:7; John 14:1–6). According to Jesus, keeping calm involves keeping a prophetic perspective. Knowing the best is to come breeds a sense of peace and security in the Christian heart and home.

With our need to have a view of the future informed by Jesus and not our emotions or the latest disturbing headline, we would do well to turn to the Olivet Discourse as we find it recorded in Mark 13:1–37.

There is an old saying, "If you want to find out what happened yesterday read the newspaper; if you want to discover what happened today, watch the six-o'clock news; if you want to know what going to happen tomorrow, read the Bible." That observation is true. And there is no better place in the Bible than the Olivet Discourse to encounter a concise and clear panoramic view of the future and the last days leading up to Jesus's triumphant return.

Pivoting off a question about the destruction of the Temple in Jerusalem (fulfilled AD 70), Jesus opened a window into the more distant future and the dark unrepeatable days of the Great Tribulation immediately leading up to His return in judgement, power, and glory (Mark 13:13:1–4, 5–8, 14–23, 24–27). The words of the Lord Jesus here have been called "The Mini Apocalypse" because they form a concise—a kind of Readers Digest—version of the end times. There are themes and truths pressed together here to be found in large sections of the prophecies Daniel, Ezekiel, Zechariah, and the book of Revelation. Of particular note is the fact Jesus preached this message on the last days and His second advent from the very spot to which He will return (Mark 13:3; Zech. 14:1–4; Acts 1:10–11).

Let's now take a look at this pivotal prophetic passage and allow it to form a protective shield in our lives against the onslaught of fear regarding the future. This discourse would remind us to look out is to be distressed but to look up is to be blessed.

THE PICTURE JESUS EMPLOYS

In describing the signs to take place on the earth before the world witnesses the signs in the heavens prior to His triumphant return, Jesus employs and utilizes a dramatic and rather revealing image (Mark 13:5–8, 24–27). Christ describes some of the events leading up to His unveiling from heaven as "the beginning of sorrows" (Mark 13:8). Literally "the beginning of birth pains." Embedded in this image is the thought that just before the delivery of God's kingdom on earth and the eternal state, the world will first squirm and squeal in sorrow like a mother in labor (1 Thess. 5:3). The days prior to Jesus's revelation from heaven will be marked by the sorrows of spiritual deception, natural disasters, famines, social upheaval, and internal conflict centered on the Middle East (Mark 13:5–8).

The reason I say international conflict (wars and rumors of wars) centered on the Middle East is because of the Jewish flavor of this discourse. Jesus's focus on the future is focused on the Jewish people, Judea, and the temple in Jerusalem. He speaks of the sabbath (Mark 13:20); He speaks of fleeing Judea (Mark 13:14); and He speaks of the desecration of the Holy Place (Mark 13:15; Matt. 24:15). According to the Word incarnate, Israel and the Middle East is the magnet pulling together the events of the last days.

By way of further explanation, these sorrows described by the Lord Jesus in the opening part of the Olivet Discourse are only the beginning of the world's woes (Mark 13:8). These are the signature events preceding and bumping up against the time of Great Tribulation, a time of unparalleled and unrepeatable horror and destruction within history (Mark 13:19–20; Matt. 24:21–22). And these signs or signature events just like birth pains will increase in intensity and frequency in the days leading up to the tribulation period and the second advent of the Savior.

The thing we must underscore in our thinking is Jesus does not see the world ascending to utopia but descending into pandemonium. The United Nations will fail in its mission. Men will be unable to restore Eden. Science will not fix the human condition bedeviled by sin. The Olivet Discourse tells us it gets worse before it gets better. Just as the darkest part of the night is just before dawn, so within history some of earth's darkest hours will be just before the dawning of the Bright and Morning Star (Rev. 22:16). Theologically speaking there will be no peace on earth, no détente, until the Prince of Peace returns and reigns (Isa. 9:6–7). It is Jesus's return to earth and His reign on earth at the end of history that secures the future and restores paradise lost (Rev. 19–22).

I like what Ray Stedman says about the fact that in the book of Revelation we see history come full circle with the effects of the fall reversed and paradise restored by means of Jesus' return and the creation of a new heaven and a new earth. He writes:

> Someone has rightly observed that the book of Genesis and the book of Revelation are like two bookends that hold the entire Bible together. In Genesis we have the story of the origin of human sin; in Revelation we have the complete and final victory over sin. Genesis presents the beginning of human history and civilization; Revelation presents the end of both. In Genesis we learn the beginnings of God's judgment and His grace toward mankind; in Revelation we see the awesome result of His judgment and the triumph of His grace. The great themes of these two books are intricately intertwined.[1]

A nearsighted view of the world is grim and dim, but a farsighted view is laden with hope and the promise of peace. The near future is marked by sorrow and a very ugly chapter in human history, but beyond lies the Second Coming and a world in which there is no crying, no sighing, and no dying (Rev. 21:4). So as far as this old world of ours is concerned, weeping may endure for a night, but joy will suddenly and surely come in the morning when Jesus comes back (Psa. 30:5). When Jesus comes, the curse will be reversed (Rev. 22:3), death will be put to death (Rev. 20:14), all things will be made new (Rev. 21:5), Satan will be banished (Rev. 20:10), the sinner will be punished (Rev. 22:15), the righteous will be rewarded (Rev. 22:14), God Almighty will be worshipped (Rev. 21:22–24; 22:3), and Jesus will be exalted as our Lord and sacrificial Lamb (Rev. 21:22–23). In the end we win!

In March of 2009, I found myself preaching at a beautiful retreat center in North Carolina called the Cove. It is owned and run by the Billy Graham Evangelistic Association. While there I visited a kind of chapel that presented in photos and words a mosaic of the ministry of Billy Graham. In one of the photos and presentations, I read about a time when Dr. Graham was summoned to 10 Downing Street in London to meet Winston Churchill. Churchill pointed to the newspaper headlines and asked, "What hope do you have for the world?" The young evangelist took his New Testament and said, "I am filled with hope!" Then he proceeded to preach the death, burial, resurrection, and Second Coming of Christ. Churchill listened and then replied, "I do not see much hope for the future unless it is the hope you are talking about young man."

Today's newspaper headlines are not any better. The world is marked by terrorism, the disintegration of the family, racial and ethnic tensions, environmental disturbance, unstable markets, the specter of nuclear catastrophe, and wars in the Middle East with world-wide ramifications. What hope is there? It is the hope preached by Billy Graham to Winston Churchill, a hope centered on the promised return of Christ at the end of human history with the goal of reversing the fall and restoring Eden on earth. That is a wonderful hope to take cover under. For those without Christ there is trouble ahead, but for the Christian there is triumph ahead (2 Cor. 2:14).

THE PARTICULARS JESUS EXPLAINS

Like runway lights facilitating an airplane's approach and safe landing, Jesus in the Olivet Discourse gives us a series of signs lighting the future and announcing His demonstrable arrival. According to Jesus, His visible and victorious return will be telegraphed by certain events and emergencies. During the last years of human history, the atmosphere will be thick with a foreboding sense of the climactic and catastrophic. Men's hearts will fail them for fear as they watch the unfolding events of the last days (Luke 21:26).

To make His point, Jesus speaks in parable form of the budding of the fig tree (Mark 13:28–30). Just as the blossoming of the fig tree with its buds turning into leaves indicates summer is near, so the events described by Jesus here in Mark 13 will be a clear indication His return is at hand (Mark 13:29; Phil. 4:5; James 5:8). Just as the coming of spring announces the coming of summer, so the beginning of sorrows and the days of tribulation will announce Jesus has risen from His throne in heaven and is on His way back to earth (Mark 13:8, 19, 24).

It is important to note the signs announced by Jesus are spread out over a period of time. There are signs leading up to the time of horrible tribulation (Mark 13:5–13). There are signs surrounding the great tribulation (Mark 13:14–23). And there are signs announcing the unveiling of Christ at the Second Coming (Mark 13:24–27). Some of the signs will take place on earth and some of the signs will take place in the heavens. Either way there are early signs, then essential signs, and then end signs. When Jesus returns to earth nobody will be able to say, "Why wasn't I told about this?"

According to Jesus the last days will be marked by:

- False Christ's and gospels (Mark 13:6, 21–23)
- Wars and rumors of wars (Mark 13:7–8)
- Famines as a result of war (Mark 13:8)
- Earthquakes and natural disasters (Mark 13:8)
- Persecution of the righteous (Mark 13:9, 11–13)
- Global missions (Mark 13:10)
- Desecration of the Temple (Mark 13:14)
- Great tribulation (Mark 13:14–20)
- Cosmic chaos (Mark 13:24–27)

At this point I want to add a big footnote. It would seem from a reading of the text these signs will unfold in the space of a generation.

Jesus says, "this generation will by no means pass away till all these things take place" (Mark 13:30). In all likelihood Christ is speaking about the generation of people who will witness the beginning of sorrows, the Tribulation and the coming of Christ in glory within the span of several years. If that is the case, it is important for us to deduce from the Olivet Discourse, Jesus is not describing general conditions throughout history or the church age but the final days of earth leading to the finale, the unveiling of Christ at the Parousia. Strictly speaking then we should not expect to see any major fulfillment of these events or emergencies in our day.

This teaching by Christ in the Olivet Discourse fundamentally refers to Israel, the world, and the Tribulation period. We noted earlier the Jewish flavor of this passage. That being true, it is my conviction the church has a distinct destiny from Israel and the world at large and will not be on earth during this time of unparalleled trouble. Along with many Christians, I believe the Church will be raptured and removed to heaven as Jesus promised in John's gospel and the book of the Revelation and as Paul taught in his letter to the Thessalonians (John 14:1–6; 1 Thess. 1:10, 4:13–18, 5:1–11; Rev. 3:10–11). As my friend and prophecy expert Mark Hitchcock notes:

None of the key New Testament passages that deal with the Tribulation mention the presence of the church. The primary section in the Bible that describes the Tribulation period is Revelation 4–19. In these chapters there is a curious silence about the church. In Revelation 1–3 the church is specially mentioned nineteen times. It is again mentioned in Revelation 22:16. But between those two points, the church of Jesus Christ is strangely absent from the biblical account of events on the earth. To me this is strong evidence that the church will not be present on earth during the Tribulation.[2]

There is a distinction to be made between the Rapture and the Revelation. In the Rapture, Jesus comes for the Church prior to the Tribulation, and the movement is from earth to heaven (John 14:1–6; 1 Thess. 4:13–18), while in the Revelation, Jesus comes with His church after the Tribulation, and the movement is from heaven to earth (Jude 14; Rev.

19:6–14). After the Rapture the Tribulation begins (2 Thess. 1:6–9), while after the Revelation the Millennial kingdom begins (Rev. 20:1–7). At the Rapture, the saved are delivered from wrath (1 Thess. 1:10, 5:9), while at the Revelation the unsaved face the wrath of God (Rev. 6:12–17). Bottom line, in this distinction between the Rapture and the Revelation, the Church is shown to be in the Father's House with Christ during the Tribulation.[3]

If that is the case, we would do well to temper our enthusiasm for connecting prophetic dots. We must not shout "eureka" with every headline in the News that seems to match the prophetic Scriptures. The signs outlined by Jesus in the Olivet Discourse clearly await the period of the Tribulation, and their fulfillment will be compressed into a generation alive at the time. By implication, the Church ought to be Savior watching not sign watching (1 Thess. 1:10; Phil. 3:20–21; Titus 2:13; Jude 21). The church is to await the advent of Christ not the Antichrist. The Rapture in distinction from the Revelation is sudden, imminent, and without signs; therefore, we ought to be looking up more than looking out.

That said it is possible we might see what prophetic scholars call "stage setting." While the church age is not a time in which we expect to see major prophetic fulfillment, that is not to say in our time God may not be preparing the world for a time beyond the Church age. We might witness some prophetic overlap. It is not beyond the realm of possibility to see events in our day trending toward events described in the Olivet Discourse and other significant prophetic passages. Just as history was prepared for the first advent of Christ, in a similar way history will be prepared for the second advent of Christ. Galatians 4:4 tells us Jesus came the first time, "when the fullness of time had come," which means during a time within history ripened and made ready by the providence of God. The same will be true when Jesus comes a second time. As Tommy Ice notes, "Just as many people set their clothes out the night before they wear them the following day, so in the same sense God is preparing the world for the certain fulfillment of prophecy in a future time."[4]

It is possible the signs of our times will point in the direction of the signs of the end times. We may well witness some "stage setting" in our day that declares the world is further tilting toward the Revelation of Jesus Christ from heaven. What we are seeing in our day with the revival of the Roman Empire in Europe, global money markets, Israel in the land, disputes over Jerusalem and the Temple, the moral conditions like the days of Lot and Noah, the disintegration of the home, hedonism, theological apostasy, and cold indifference in the church may well be a foreshadowing of the days leading up to the day of judgment. And if true, one wonders how near the Rapture might we be? If we are seeing things trending toward end time prophecy, events after the Rapture, how close must the Rapture be?

Again, as I said earlier, the Church must be Savior watching not sign watching. We must live on tip toes of expectancy regarding Jesus's coming to the air for His Church. Just recently my wife June was helping in our Special Needs Ministry at church, a ministry run by our daughter Beth. One of the girls we minister to, Ramona, said to her, "Mrs. De Courcy, I am ready." Not exactly sure what she meant, June asked, "What are you ready for?" Without batting an eyelid Ramona replied. "I am ready to see Jesus." How wonderful. Oh, that you and I would live like that. Oh, that we would get our eyes off ourselves and our circumstances, off the present day with all its bad news, and fix them on the coming of Christ for His church (Titus 2;13). May we live this day in the light of "that day" (2 Tim. 1:12).

THE PREPAREDNESS JESUS EMPHASIZES

To study the Olivet Discourse is to discover a call to action. The sermon is peppered with nineteen imperatives, nineteen commanding commitments. For example, people are told to take heed, do not worry, speak, endure, flee, watch, and pray (Mark 13:5, 11–12, 13, 14, 33). As Jesus preaches His longest discourse in Mark's Gospel, which is on prophecy, He makes it practical. Jesus understands as do the other biblical writers that prophecy is not given by God to satisfy our curiosity but to direct our behavior and shape our lives. It has been given to make us more hardy, holy, and hopeful (James 5:7–8; 1 John 3:3; Titus 2:13). In the best circumstances, the study of prophetic Scripture acts as a stimulant not a sedative in the Christian life. A look into the future fits us not only for the next life but for this life. That is why the study of prophecy must never be a dead end but a path to greater service, wider witness, longer obedience, and deeper intimacy with Christ.

We would do well to heed the warning of Dr. David Jeremiah as he writes about this very danger in his book *Jesus' Final Warning.* With insight he writes and warns:

You may know how many toes there are on the beast in Daniel's vision. You may have memorized intricate charts on the book of Revelation. You may have twenty-seven theories on how to calculate the number of the Antichrist. But to know all that and not have the message come home to your heart is to be subtlety sent down a cul-de-sac. It may even cause you—or others—to miss the highway to heaven.[5]

This emphasis on ethical eschatology and practical prophecy is Jesus' emphasis. The study of prophecy must never become a theological cul-de-sac. Jesus tells the final generation to be awake and alert concerning His return to recapture earth, which lies under the sway of the devil (1 John 5:19). They need to be cognizant of the unfolding events as Jesus predicted, and just as flowers in spring tell you summer is near, so the signs outlined by Christ in the Olivet Discourse will tell them His coming is close (Mark 13:28–31).

Changing metaphors and moving from the outdoors to the indoors, Jesus imagines an owner about to leave on a long trip instructing his servants concerning their duties in his absence and the need for them to remain faithful and watchful. It would not do for the master to return and find them unfaithful and sleeping (Mark 13:32–37). They must be on guard, they must always act in the context of their master's anticipated return. And so, it is with Christ and His followers. His absence and promised return should breed faithfulness not unfaithfulness and work not laziness.

At significant points throughout this discourse, the Lord Christ calls on the final generation to "take heed" and "watch out" (Mark 13:5, 9, 23, 33–34, 35, 37). This is not a passive waiting, like standing at a bus stop, but an active waiting, like working hard until the factory horn blows. This is a call to His final followers to maintain steadfast faith and costly obedience. They were to be watchful through theological discernment in the face of false teachers and teaching (Mark 13:5–6, 22–23). They were to be watchful through gospel proclamation and public witness (Mark 13:10–11). They were to be watchful through perseverance in the face of persecution (Mark 13:12–13), and they were to be watchful through prayerful dependence upon God (Mark 13:33).

What is to be true of that final generation must also be true of our generation. The Church must be watchful (Rom. 13:11–14; 1 Thess. 1:10; 5:4–8). In 1 Thessalonians 1:10, Paul uses a word translated "wait" that means to "remain up." It is the idea of waiting up in expectation. It is the picture of a mother waiting up for the return of a child late in the evening. It is the picture of a child waiting up for Christmas morning. It is the picture of a girl waiting up for the arrival of her boyfriend at any moment. It is a word that speaks of excited and intense expectation. The church ought to be living on its tip-toes looking for the blessed hope and glorious return of Christ.

Like those in a future day, we ought to be watchful through theological discernment in the face of false teachers and teaching (1 Tim. 4:1–2; 2 Tim. 4:3–4; 1 John 4:1). We also ought to be watchful through gospel proclamation and public witness (Matt. 28:18–20; Acts 1:8–9), watchful through perseverance in the face of persecution (Acts 14:22; Phil. 1:29; 1 Peter 4;12–19), and watchful through prayerful dependence upon God (1 Peter 4:7–10; Rev. 22:20).

Study the New Testament, and you will not find the church or the followers of Christ being admonished to set dates, pinpoint the Antichrist, identify the False Prophet, or profile the Four Horsemen of the Apocalypse. Rather, the church is constantly called to ethical eschatology, to practical prophecy, to a manner of life focused on prayer, evangelism, church service, family life, hard work, and godliness. A love for

Jesus's appearing will invariably lead the Christian to greater love of life, love of family, love of neighbor, love of the church, and greater love for the lost (2 Tim. 4:8). Remember the doctrine of the Second Coming is not a spiritual sedative; it is rather a spiritual stimulant that gives purpose and passion to the meantime while we wait for the end time.

Growing up in Northern Ireland, I remember my Pastor Ivan Thompson telling the story of a fishing fleet from a village in Scotland heading home. They had been out to sea for several weeks. As they returned, the village gathered at the docks to welcome the boys home. On one of the vessels, the captain looking through his spyglass informed some of the crew, "John, I see your Mary," "James, I see your mother is there," "William, I see your Catherine and the two boys." One man by the name of Angus asked the captain if he saw his wife on the dock. The captain looked one more time but informed Angus his wife was not there. So, when the boats docked, Angus looked anxiously for his wife but to no avail. Not being able to find her, he made his way sluggishly up the hill to their cottage. In entering the home his wife greeted him with a kiss and said, "Oh, Angus, I have been waiting for you!" Not hiding his disappointment Angus replied, "Ah, but the rest of the wives were watching."

Are we waiting passively for Jesus or are we watching actively for Jesus? May we begin each day with the thought "Perhaps Today!" May we not be found sleeping at our post when the Master returns! Listen to the words of Christ, "Therefore you also be ready, for the Son of Man is coming at an hour you do not expect" (Matt. 24:44).

In a world hurtling toward Armageddon, may we take cover in the enduring and exciting hope we find for ourselves as God's people in the promised return of Jesus. Our future is as bright as the promise of God is sure! The best is yet to come!

CHAPTER 6

SEND FOR THE POLICE

TAKING COVER IN A LIFE GUARDED BY LAWFUL GOVERNMENT PROTECTIONS

*The rights of persons, and the rights of property,
are the objects, for the protection of which
Government was instituted.*

James Madison

The Methodists gathered for a state-wide camp meeting, which headlined some of their finest preachers. Before things got going, one of their featured speakers called in sick. He communicated he would not be there to preach his assigned sermon. In response the senior minister presiding over the event pulled a young minister aside into the camp office and said, "I want you to preach right after lunch today." The young preacher by now breaking a sweat replied, "What am I going to preach? I didn't bring a sermon with me. I am not prepared. What am I going to preach?"

In a condescending manner and with a pious voice the lead pastor said, "Just trust the Lord, young man. Just trust the Lord."

The young preacher was desperate. Not knowing what to do, he remained in the camp office pondering his next move. While there he noticed a Bible sitting on a shelf in front of him and so he picked it up and began leafing through it for a text. In turning the pages of this Bible, he came across a set of typed notes that were obviously a sermon. Delighted by what he read, he took the notes and preached them straight after lunch. The sermon was a hit. The crowd thrilled to this young man's preaching and showered him with glowing commendations at the end of the service. Everyone seemed impressed except for the camp leader. He hurriedly pushed his way through the crowd and confronted the young man. He thundered, "Young man, you preached my sermon, the sermon I was going to give tonight in the closing session. Now what am I going to do?" The young man looked him straight in the face and in solemn tones replied, "Just trust the Lord. Just trust the Lord."[1]

As this humorous story illustrates, trusting the Lord does not mean you do nothing, or ignore your responsibility, or fail to look to others for help. Looking to God for help does not equate to blind trust or a kind of fatalism that excuses us from thinking hard, acting wisely, or leaning on others for help, wisdom, or protection. We ought not forget, while God works directly apart from human agency, He also and often works indirectly through human agency. Oliver Cromwell was right when he famously said to his troops in the English Civil War, "Trust God and keep your powder dry."

To study Scripture is to be confronted with a balanced view of trusting God and acting prudently. Nehemiah and the inhabitants of Israel prayed to God for protection in the face of their enemies, but they also posted guards along the walls of Jerusalem (Neh. 4:14–23). David went up against Goliath in the name of the living God, but he still took his slingshot and stones with him (1 Sam. 17:47–49). The disciples learned to trust God for everything and in all circumstances, yet at Jesus' word, they bought and carried swords for self-protection (Luke 22:35–38). These biblical examples illustrate trusting God and keeping your powder dry. The use of means, the employment of our own initiative, the help of others need not lessen our faith in God.

Trusting God must therefore never lead to testing God with impractical ideas or reckless actions or the twisting of God's promises as we see happen in the temptations presented by Satan to Christ in the wilderness (Matt. 4:5–7). Trusting God does not deny the natural, the human, or practical side of life.

In the context of our study on finding peace and security, we would do well to remind ourselves it is not a lack of trust in God on the part of Christians to look to civil authorities for protection. Within the wise providence of God, He has provided human government as a means of protection and security for His people and all people. It is the government's God-given responsibility to protect the lawful and good citizen while at the same time punishing the evildoer (Rom. 13:3–5). Governments that fulfill their God-given duties will be a refuge for lawful citizens seeking justice and protection. As a servant of God, the government can within the providence of God serve the servants of God in the realm of public order (Rom. 13:6).

The apostle Paul was a man who trusted God unswervingly and without reserve (2 Tim. 1:12). This was a man whose life testified to the fact he was shipwrecked on God. Yet, in the light of what I have just said, it is instructive to note Paul's trust in God did not preclude him from seeking the protection of the government when appropriate. Study the book of Acts, and you will see him exercise his political rights as a Roman citizen and seek protection under the law. As a soldier of Jesus Christ, he was more than happy on several occasions to be guarded by Roman soldiers when expedient. Paul took cover in governmental protections on more than one occasion as he went about the business of serving Jesus Christ (Acts 16:37–39, 22:25–29, 23:12–27, 25:10–11). From Luke's account of early church history in the book of Acts, we see Paul's commitment to serve Jesus Christ sacrificially did not include the wanton abandonment of his civil rights and government protections under the law. This apostle to the Gentiles was willing to suffer for the cause of the Gospel, but as we see in his call for government protection he was not willing to suffer needlessly.

As modern-day followers of Paul and the Lord Jesus Christ, we need to listen and learn and therefore take cover in a life guarded when necessary by civil courts, law enforcement, and military forces. The government of the United States as "God's minister" can be within the wise and kind providence of God the means by which God brings a greater measure of security to His people. The God who governs governments can employ them in the service of His kingdom for the benefit and protection of His people.

To that end, let's take an excursion into the biblical text and learn about God's design for government and how government in the best circumstances can serve our good and be a means of God-directed justice and protection (Prov. 29:4; Rom. 13:3; 1 Peter 2;14).

THE NEXUS OF GOVERNMENT

To begin, we need to connect the emergence and role of human government within the plan and purpose of God. According to the Bible, government was God's idea. The God who governs all things has established human government to be a means by which life is better maintained, ordered, and enhanced (Rom. 13:1; 1 Peter 2:13). Jesus made it clear in talking to Pilate that governmental authority has been delegated from God and comes from above (John 19:11). Human government in an ultimate sense does not find its legitimacy in evolutionary inevitability, the ballot box, or the will of domineering men, but in God. From heaven's perspective, it is God who decides who is in power. It is God from a higher throne who sets kingdoms up and pulls kingdoms down (Prov. 21:1; Dan. 2:20–21, 44; 4:25–26, 32).

My friend and mentor John MacArthur is helpful here as he comments on Romans 13:1:

> In whatever form its exists, government and its authority derive directly from God and exists to benefit society. Like marriage, government is a universal institution that is valid regardless of place, circumstance, or other consideration.[2]

What this means is under the sovereignty of God governments have the divine right to exist and to exercise a certain rule over their people, for the good of their people. After all, "there is no authority except from God, and the authorities that exist are appointed by God" (Rom. 13:1). To be sure men will abuse and misuse this divine institution and its power, but that does not mean the role and rule of government as a whole is bad or to be rejected. In the best circumstances, government will act as "God's minister" for the general protection, peace, progress, and prosperity of its people (Prov. 29:2; Rom. 13:1–7; 1 Peter 2:13–14).

That being the case we would do well to remind ourselves that failure to submit to governmental authority, pay our taxes, and show respect to government offices and officers is an act of treason against heaven. I say that because God commands us to do all three (Titus 3:1; Mark 12:13–17; Rom. 13:6–7). The Christian ought to be a model citizen (1 Peter 2:13–17).

A qualification however must be made. The biblical call to submission and obedience is not unlimited. Nowhere in the Bible are we called as followers of Christ to give blind obedience to men. We are not to be "submissive as dogs" as Hilter described many protestants in Nazi Germany during World War II.[3] The state is God-ordained, but it is not sovereign; God alone is sovereign. Consequently, we must always obey God and His word before the statues of human governments or civil authorities. It is God's kingdom we seek first (Matt. 6:33). It was the apostles of Christ who stated when censored by civil authorities, "We ought to obey God rather than men" (Acts 5:29). In fact, the Holy Scriptures outline five areas of legitimate civil disobedience on the part of God's people

- When the worship of God is prohibited (Ex. 5:1–2)
- When the murder of the innocent is sanctioned (Ex. 1:15–21)
- When an act of idolatry is required (Dan. 3:1–7; 6:6–9)
- When evangelism is censored (Acts 4:17–20)
- When the culture deifies man (Rev. 13:4, 8)

The Christian's obedience to the state is contingent and limited. We report to a higher throne first and foremost. The Bible could not be clearer. We are to obey the state until obedience to the state would lead to disobedience to God.

In speaking about civil disobedience, it is often the case the government exceeds its place and power. While the government has a God-given role to play, it must see itself within a nexus of spheres, realms, and domains of God-given authority. Theologically speaking, this nexus involves and includes the state, the church, and the home. Each one independent of the other and yet interdependent on each other. Each benefits the other; each is to be complementary not contrary. Jesus recognizes this idea and ideal of separation of powers and authority when he states, "Render therefore to Caesar the things that are Caesar's and to God the things that are God's" (Matt. 22:21).

The family is the most basic of all divine institutions. God started history with a heterosexual marriage and family and intended for it to become the building block of a strong society and healthy culture (Gen. 2:23–25). God has invested authority in parents to raise their children to love God and love their neighbor (Eph. 6:1–4). Next to the family, God instituted human government following the fall and the flood. God's purpose for government was to act as a bulwark against man's sin nature and its societal effects such as disorder, depravity, and death. Here God invested authority in human government to preserve order and where necessary take the lives of those threatening the lives of others (Gen. 9:5–6; Rom. 13:1–7). And next to the family and government, God established the church and invested it with authority to proclaim the good news of the gospel of Jesus Christ (Matt. 28:18–20). It is the church's job to go throughout the world and make disciples of all nations. In God's world, in simple terms, it is the government's job to protect and preserve life, it is the family's job to raise the next generation, and it is the church's job to offer the shining hope of Jesus Christ for this life and the next.

Without going too deeply, it is of vital importance that men and women respect the God-given functions of each institution. When these various spheres function side by side, law and order is preserved, family life and generational continuity is advanced, and God's blessing through the gospel of the Lord Jesus enriches countries, cultures, and couples. However, disruption comes when leadership in one sphere trespasses into the other. History tells us the marriage of church and state has never been a healthy one. History tells us the government cannot raise the next generation or replace the family. History shows when the church fails to be gospel-centered it loses its impact and relevancy.

Again, that is why we see the apostles refuse to obey the civil authorities in Acts 5:29. Why? Because they determined the civil authorities had no authority to tell them to stop preaching when Christ gave them authority to do just that. The moment the state stepped out of its circle of influence, it lost its influence.

Each sphere is intended and designed to be a help to the other. The government can create the circumstances for the family to flourish. Strong families are a blessing to the church and the society. The church can come alongside the family and help raise children in the fear and admonition of the Lord. The church can also act as the conscience of the nation. Each sphere can help the other, but failure to respect their God-given callings and authority creates the potential of each harming the other. A biblical worldview enthusiastically embraces limited government, strong families with mothers and fathers at the helm, and a vibrant and vocal church strong in its witness to the gospel of Jesus Christ.

The story is told of a sea captain and his chief engineer who liked to argue over whose job on the ship was the most important. To settle this conflict once and for all, they decided to swap places. The chief engineer climbed to the bridge, while the captain descended to the engine room.

Several hours later the captain suddenly appeared on deck covered in oil and grim. Waving his monkey wrench at the bridge he yelled to the chief engineer, "You have to get down there. I can't make her go!" The chief engineer quickly replied, "Of course you can't. I have run the ship aground."[4]

Piggy backing off this story, the same disastrous results befall a nation when the spheres of government, home, and the church start competing with each other instead of complementing each other. Things run aground when the nexus of government is not respected.

THE NECESSITY OF GOVERNMENT

G. K. Chesterton, the English essayist, is reported to have said, "Seemingly from the dawn of man all nations have had governments, and all nations have been ashamed of them." Ronald Reagan in a speech before the US Chamber of Commerce in 1972 said, "In some dim beginning, man created the institution of government as a convenience to himself. And ever since that time, government has been doing its best to become an inconvenience."[5] Whether good or bad, whether we like them or not, governmental bodies have been with us from the beginnings of history. Government has been a universal reality in all cultures and countries across the world, and across time. While they may have come in different shapes and sizes, big government or limited government, monarchical government or parliamentary, democratic government or theocratic, nations have rarely if ever been without some form of government. The emergence and existence of human government has been universal, continuous, and apparently necessary.

It has been that way for at least two reasons. One reason being man's creation, and the other being man's corruption.

Human Government and Man's Creation

I think it is true to say ruling is an instinctual thing with mankind. I believe a fact often overlooked in our discussions on government is the reality that at the point of creation God made man in His image and gave him dominion over the natural and animal world (Gen. 1:26–28). As the crown of God's creation, man became God's representative on earth in expressing and enacting divine rule over creation. The command to exercise dominion over the earth and all living creatures separated and elevated mankind from the rest of creation (Psa. 8:6). Man is below God as His creature, but as one made in the image of God and one made for friendship with God, man is above the rest of creation. Uniquely, man within creation was called to govern the world above, beneath, and around him in compliance with the will and purpose of the Creator.

One of the big takeaways from our theology of creation is it helps explain the historical phenomena of government. Government is clearly a manifestation of the image of God in man. Man's instinct for the necessity of government is a consequence of his being made after the image of a ruling God. Man is a governing being by nature.

Human Government and Man's Corruption

Continuing this train of thought on the necessity of human government is not to be seen only in the fact man is a governing being, but he is also a guilty being. Through Adam's disobedience and fall from grace, man has existed in a state of rebellion against God (Rom. 3:10–18, 23; 5:12). Just like Adam in his choices, mankind has sought to displace God from the center of life (Rom. 1:18–32). According to the apostle John the world is in a state of lawlessness (1 John 3:4).

The sad reality is man created by God to exercise dominion over the earth under God is now apart from the grace of God under the dominion of sin resulting in disobedience, disorder, and death (Rom. 6:12–14; 7:17–23). Outside Christ, men and women are slaves to sin and under the dominion of death. Sin has tied man in knots and strangled human happiness (Prov. 5:22).

Because of Adam's fall and rejection of God's authority, mankind now lives in a world crippled by chaos and conflict. Read Genesis 4–6, and you will find cataloged the sins of fratricide, bigamy, violence, and demonic immorality. Things got so bad God regretted making mankind, so bad He decided to send a great flood to cleanse the earth of every living soul except Noah and his family (Gen. 6–7).

Of interest to us is the fact that, following the judgement of God in the great flood, we see God inaugurating human government with punitive powers as a restraint against sin in the future. In a covenant with Noah and his descendants (all of us), God allowed for capital punishment in the case of murder (Gen. 9:5–6). Remember the earth was filled with violence prior to the flood, and now God is requiring a reckoning for the crime of murder (Gen. 6:13). This reckoning was to be administered by other human beings acting justly and with divine sanction. And by implication and extension, the imposition of lesser punishments for lesser crimes would seem natural and necessary.

The point I really want to underscore is at this juncture in human history civil government has an element of punishment attached to it. Man needs to be restrained, and one of the core purposes of government is to punish the wrongdoer in the pursuit of maintaining order in a fallen world. This truth of just punishment at the hands of the government is laced throughout Scripture as is found in the comments of King Solomon (Eccles. 8:11), the confession of the thief on the cross (Luke 23:40–41), and the teaching of the apostles Paul and Peter (Rom. 13:2–4; 1 Peter 2:13–14).

The tragedy of the human condition is man, created to govern and exercise dominion over the earth under God, now because of sin, needs to be governed harshly. By deduction I believe it is fair to say when man seeks to throw off the restraint of government in acts of anarchy he is simply evidencing his innate rebellion against God. Government is a reminder of man's fallenness and lack of submission to government a reminder also.

You might consider government a necessary evil, but according to the Bible, it is necessary because of evil. Man, in his fallenness needs restraining, and government exists within God's will to act as a bulwark against the lawless expression of that fallenness. Man is not some morally neutral figure; he is corrupt, conceited, and cruel. From birth his bias is toward sin, lawlessness, and wickedness (Psa. 51:5; 58:3; Isa. 53:6). He must be protected against himself and the harm he can bring to others. That restraint comes in several forms: (1) the conscience and the law of God written on the heart (Gen. 3:22; Rom. 2:15); (2) the family and parental correction (Prov. 13:24, 19:18, 23:13); (3) the church indwelt by the Holy Spirit acting as salt and light through the gospel (Matt. 5:13–16; Phil. 2:15–16); and (4) the civil authorities in their wielding of the sword of justice (Rom. 13:1–7; 1 Pet. 2:13–14).

It is clear human government and civil authorities are to act as a restraint and retardant in a fallen world. Governments exist fundamentally because evil exists.

According to Craig Brian Larson in the early 1990s, the leaning Tower of Pisa began to lean too far. Engineers, concerned the 180-foot-high tower might soon list to a point of great danger, set about devising a system to salvage the famous landmark by holding the lean constant.

First, the engineers stabilized the ground around the tower by injecting cold liquid nitrogen into the ground to freeze it and thereby largely preventing any dangerous ground vibrations during the project. The second phase involved installing a network of underground cables that would steady the tower and pull it toward center by at least an inch.

In making application Craig Brian Larson notes, "Left to itself, our world resembles the leaning tower of Pisa: tilting and heading to catastrophe. To prevent total anarchy God establishes governments to maintain order. Governments and their laws function like steel cables that will hold the leaning tower. The tower still leans. It is not perfect. But the cables prevent total destruction."[6]

THE NATURE OF GOVERNMENT

In the need for government, we discover the nature of government. Having already touched on the protective and punitive purposes of government in the face of innate human fallenness, I want to double down on this aspect of governance. From a biblical perspective, the role of human government is largely a law-and-order and national-security one. The balance of the Bible's teaching on the role of the civil magistrate points to a focus on the promotion of moral good, protection of life, punishing of evil, and guarding the nation against threats both domestic and foreign (Rom. 13:3–4; 1 Peter 2:13–14). At a fundamental level, this is how the government serves its people best. It seeks to punish the oppressor and defend the defenseless (Psa. 82:2–4; Prov. 31:8–9; Dan. 4:27). Failure to protect those in danger, failure to punish the evil doer within the country, and failure to guard the nation from outside threats is a dereliction of a government's God-given duty.

C. S. Lewis speaks eloquently to this when he writes:

> It is easy to think the State has a lot of different objects— military, political, economic, and what not. But in a way things are much simpler than that. The State exists simply to promote and to protect the ordinary happiness of human beings in this life. A husband and wife chatting over a fire, a couple of friends having a game of darts in a pub, a man reading a book in his own room or digging in his own garden— that is what the State is there for. And unless they are helping to increase and prolong and protect such moments, all the laws, parliaments, armies, courts, police, economics, etc., are simply a waste of time.[7]

To see this role with greater clarity let's take a closer look at Romans 13:1–7, a passage we have quoted several times already. Several things jump out at us from the text about the government's role in the promotion of the good and the prevention of the bad.

First, government has been appointed by God and is to act as His minister (Rom. 13:4, 6; 1 Peter 2:14). Interestingly, the term "minister" used here by Paul is the same Greek word used by Paul elsewhere to describe the office of deacon in the church (Phil. 1:1; 1 Tim. 3:8–13). Human governments in the best circumstances is to act like any good deacon, which means they will act in the humble service of God and others. And the expression of their humble service toward God and others focuses on the promotion of the general good within society by the eradication and punishment of those who practice evil and lawlessness.

By implication, the image of government as "God's minister" says two things to us. On the one hand, it is a reminder for all to view government as a gift from God and that which benefits mankind. As Christians, we should be cheering for government to succeed and working within government to make it work for the people. On the other hand, it is a reminder there is no such a thing as a secular state. Governments are appointed by God, and if they are self-aware they will seek to serve His purposes within the world by promoting good and punishing evil. God will hold nations accountable to himself (Dan. 4:17). Kings and kingdoms that forget God will be punished (Psa. 2:10–12; 9:17). There is to be no divorcing of morality and government, for God expects nations to reflect His righteous law (Prov. 14:34).

Second, government exists for the promotion of the common good (Rom. 13:3–4; 1 Peter 2:14). The basic idea here would seem to involve the thought the law-abiding citizen has nothing to fear from government, and the civil magistrate will in turn allow him to live in peace and freedom (1 Thess. 4:11). The reference to government "praising or approving" good citizens speaks to the role of government in rewarding good citizens who promote the common good (Rom. 13:3).

Theologian and writer Wayne Grudem expands:

> Some examples of the government supporting the common good would include tax-supported playgrounds and parks where families can picnic, and sports teams can practice. This responsibility to promote what is good would also provide a justification for giving tax-free status to churches on the understanding that churches generally are good for society and promote the well-being of citizens. The same principle would also provide support for government promoting marriage through certain legal privileges and economic benefits.[8]

Third, government is to be a coercive force in restraining of evil and punishing the evildoer (Rom. 13:4; 1 Peter 2:14). While commending those who do right, the government equally condemns those who do wrong. With the authority of God himself, the civil powers are to be God's "avenging angel," visiting judgment on those who step out of line regarding God's law and civil norms. This judgment is to be marked by urgency (Eccles. 8:11), impartiality (Deut. 13:6–9), equity (Deut. 19:21; 25:3), and severity (Deut. 17:12–13; 19:20).

Plainly, the government is to restrain those who are morally unrestrained, the government is to hurt those who hurt others. The civil magistrate is not to be redemptive but punitive in the face of evil doing. While the church is redemptive in its calling through the Gospel, the government is punitive in its calling. It is not to show mercy to the merciless, for it is not to "bear the sword in vain" as an agent of divine punishment (Rom. 13:4).

Government ought not to be indecisive or passive or shrink back from actions that might include taking life in the pursuit of preserving life and the advancement of justice. The image of the "sword" includes the idea of capital punishment. In a previous passage Paul, used the image of the sword to speak of death (Rom. 8:35), and throughout Scripture this image of the sword has frequently been associated with death and execution (Matt. 26:52; Acts 12:2; Rev. 13:10). Bottom line, in the extreme, the state has a God-given authority and duty to protect life by the death of those who wantonly take life. God ordained government is the divinely appointed agent of vengeance, not the citizen nor the Christian (Rom. 13:1–7; cp. Rom. 12:17–21).

Three added thoughts seem appropriate here. One, the punishment of evil does not extend to all kinds of evil. Evil actions, not unkind thoughts or improper attitudes, are to be punished. What is to be punished is that which clearly imperils the safety of society. Only God can judge the heart. Two, Christians cannot sign on to a view of government or public policy that downplays human depravity or is rooted in a utopian view of life. Good government always affirms the fallenness of man. Realistically, for good to triumph, there can never be a denial of the bad in man. And, three, government by extension must not only protect its citizens against thieves and murders within its borders but also against a multitude of thieves and robbers who come as an army to cross its borders. As with Israel of old, so today, nations have a right to wage just war on those who threaten or harm their people, freedoms, way of life, or the integrity of their national borders. Without doubt a time can come when it is necessary, just, and appropriate for a nation to go to war (Eccles. 3:8).

Trusting God's wisdom and plan for mankind involves depending on the government to shelter our families from persecution, intimidation, injustice, crime, and foreign threats.

In a world fraught with danger, we need to take cover in a life guarded by courts, law enforcement, and military defense. While our trust is ultimately in God, we need not throw away our rights as national citizens. God has tasked our governments to take care of us, and it is not a lack of faith to demand our God-given protections under the law. Faith is not impractical, unreasonable, or lacking in means.

So, let's pray for our government, judiciary, law enforcement, and military, for them to carry out their God-given duties in protecting our rights and preserving our liberties (1 Tim. 2:1–2).

So, let's use the power of the ballot box to hold our government accountable to its God-given role and responsibility (Rom. 13;1–7; 1 Peter 2:13–17). On this front, let us vote for candidates who understand the limited role of government, are pro-life in their stance, guard religious liberty, are strong on law and order, believe in capital punishment, support our troops, and are committed to protecting our borders (Prov. 11:11, 14:34, 29:2).

So, let's have our young people serve God and His kingdom through government as "God's minister" (Rom. 13:4). May we encourage them to be lawyers and judges, police officers, and military personnel. These are noble professions and professions within the providence of God established to secure our country's prosperity and peace. For example, there are numerous references to soldiers in the New Testament where military life is presented in a positive light (Luke 3:14, 14:31; Matt. 8:5–10; Luke 6:15; Acts 10–11; Heb. 11:30–40).

So, finally, let's not be embarrassed or ashamed to claim our civil rights and protections. Faith in God as we noted early in this chapter is not averse to going to court or appealing to government agencies for protection. Paul, as we noted, demanded his rights, demanded his day in court, and appealed to Roman authorities and soldiers for protection

(Acts 16:37–39, 22:25–29, 213:12–27, 25:10–11). Does anyone seriously doubt Paul's utter dependence upon God? Paul models the fact that coming to Christ and taking up your cross does not mean we have to walk away from our national privileges or protections.

Recently, I was intrigued and encouraged on this matter in reading of an episode in the life of John Paton, the nineteenth century Scottish missionary to the New Hebrides in the South Sea Islands. Any reading of this man's life will show a life marked by implicit trust in God, daring commitment to the gospel, and a life of sacrifice and service. To the uninitiated regarding his life and ministry, the tribes John Paton sought to reach for Christ where feudal in nature, violent, totally pagan, and given to cannibalism.

In 1865 John Paton along with other missionaries summoned the British authorities to address the issue of the ill-treatment of missionaries on the islands, which included the murder of some. A British man-of-war ship soon arrived and quelled the trouble, but not before firing on one of the islands and killing a handful of natives.

Some within the world of missions were aghast. John Geddie, a friend of John Paton and fellow missionary, described the events as "one of the most humiliating events in the history of modern missions." Geddie even resigned membership of a church that supported Paton.

Regardless, Paton stood his ground and along with many other missionaries felt it was the right call. Though Paton did not call for the shelling of the island, he did believe the missionaries had a right to appeal to the civil authorities for protection. He argued just as a Christian would call on the government to protect them should their house be robbed, God's servants in the New Hebrides had a right to seek the guardianship of the British Navy.

The controversy surrounding this incident meant Patton had to justify his behavior before a church body in Australia. The church authorities sought a guarantee from Paton he would not repeat his conduct in appealing to the civil authorities for protection. Paton was unwilling to make such a promise and in fact doubled down on his conviction it is a Christian's right to appeal to the government for protection against unlawful injury. He said, "I have done as clear a Christian duty as ever I did in my life. I am not ashamed. I offer no apology."[9]

I agree! Surely, the Christian is within the will of God, and within his rights to seek the protection of a legitimate government agency even in the pursuit of the work of missions. Christian faith and kingdom service does not negate our God-given protections through God-appointed ends. Therefore, you and I can take cover in a life guarded by government protections. It is a Christian thing to both trust God and send for the police!

CHAPTER 7

YOU ARE RESPONSIBLE
TAKING COVER IN A LIFE GUARDED BY SELF-DEFENSE

*It is more important to have a gun in your hand
than a cop on the phone.*

Sheriff Grady Judd

By conviction and commitment; Quakers are pacifists. They believe in hunting, but they would not kill another human being for any reason. Their philosophy is violence must be countered and conquered with nonviolence. They teach if someone were to attack them, they are to put up no resistance as it is wrong to fight or kill in self-defense. In the face of threats of physical harm, they are simply to turn the other cheek. The famous American Evangelist D. L. Moody, who was not a Quaker, said, "There has never been a time in my life when I felt that I could take a gun and shoot down a fellow being. In this aspect I am a Quaker."

Although I did read a humorous story about a wise and ingenious Quaker who was stirred awake by the noise of an intruder trying to break into his house in the middle of the night. He goes downstairs grabbing his shotgun on the way and points it at the intruder who is climbing through the window and said: "The Bible says 'Thou shalt not kill' but I want to inform you that thou art standing between me and a deer I am about to shoot."[1] As they say where there is a will there is a way.

But what about this issue of self-defense? Can a bona-fide follower of Jesus Christ protect themselves from injury at the hand of another by injuring the person who poses the threat? Can a Christian use force in the face of aggression? Can a Christian take another person's life to preserve theirs? Is there such a thing as a righteous kill? Or is a Christian bound to be a pacifist in creed and conduct, where violence is fought with the weapons of forbearance, fortitude, and forgiveness?

The question of self-defense is an important one and a pressing issue for several reasons. First, because it is a biblical issue. The Holy Scriptures directly address the issues of war, crime, and responses to personal injury. The Bible is the perfect law of God, and as such it equips us truly and thoroughly on how to handle life whether life is good, bad, or ugly (Psa. 19:7–11; 2 Tim. 3:16–17; 2 Peter 1:3). Second, because it is a practical issue. Sin has made this world a troublesome and dangerous place (Job 14:1).

Jesus talks about how wars will stain almost every page of human history (Mark 13:7–8). Paul talks about men who are quick to shed blood and how destruction and misery follow in their wake (Rom. 3:15–16). Paul also talks about his travels and the ever-present danger of being robbed (2 Cor. 11:26). Metaphorically speaking, people in general and God's people in particular are like sheep among wolves (Psa. 23:5; Matt. 10:16). Life is surrounded by danger and death. Third, because it is an American issue. American citizens are uniquely afforded a right under the Constitution to bear arms. In 2008 the Supreme Court reinforced that original right when it pronounced, "The Second Amendment protects an individual's right to possess a firearm unconnected with service with a militia, and to use that arm for traditionally lawful purposes such as self-defense within the home."[2]

Question? Is it right for the Christian to embrace that right? The Constitution of the United States may afford me the right, but does a reading of the Bible justify it? As a Christian, can I buy a gun and still look like Jesus?

It is my own conviction, one can make a solid biblical defense of self-defense. I do not believe the Bible instructs the Christian to be pacifist in the face of criminal actions and murderous intent. I do believe it is possible to kill a bad guy and remain a good guy. Owning a gun for the purposes of self-protection is not, as far as I can determine, unchristian.

That said I hasten to add this theological hot potato requires balance and humility. On the one hand, we must all agree this is a liberty of conscience issue. On the use of firearms in the matter of self-defense, we must learn to disagree with each other agreeably. It is important to remind ourselves we do not have to be identical twins on secondary matters to be brothers and sisters in Christ. As a defender of self-defense, I fully respect the sentiment expressed by Jim Elliot, the martyred missionary to the Auca Indians of Ecuador who when asked by his wife Elizabeth if he and the other four missionaries would defend themselves with guns if attacked by the Aucas, responded, "We will not use our guns. Because we are ready for heaven, but they are not."[3] Jim Elliot's position is a noble one. It is no small thing to extinguish a life made in the image of God.

On the other hand, those who advocate for the rightness of self-defense must be careful to speak with restraint. The freedom to take another life in the preservation of one's own is a grave liberty. It should never be presented in a cavalier manner. Candidly, in defending self-defense, we must not come across as "gun ho," as if we are itching to shoot someone. Gun advocates must be quick to acknowledge guns are a necessary evil to combat evil, guns are an ugly fact of life, and someday Jesus will remove them (Isa. 2:4; Joel 3:10). It is our assumption any legitimate use of a firearm in the act of self-defense is a sad but necessary response to man's fallenness.

Striking that balance and embracing those admonitions, let us now consider several questions surrounding the question of limited or lethal self-defense. The three questions I want to address are as follow: (1) Does the Bible make a defense of the right to self-defense? (2) Was Jesus a pacifist, and did He teach nonresistance in the face of violent assault? (3) Is it a lack of trust in God to own a gun?

To categorize it differently let us look at:

- The scripture question
- The savior question
- The sovereignty question

THE SCRIPTURE QUESTION

Does the Bible make a defense of the right to self-defense? As Christians, we believe the Bible is the final authority on all matters of faith and practice (2 Tim. 3:15–17). God of heaven and earth is not silent; He has spoken to us through His prophets and apostles, and supremely through His Son, Jesus Christ (Heb. 1:1–2). Therefore, in the light of the Creator's commands, we take our cue in life from the Holy Scriptures, which are God's inspired (breathed-out) words through the prophets, apostles, and the Lord Jesus Christ (Psa. 119:105, 130). It is so vital to remember the Bible not only tells us how to get to heaven but how to live justly and rightly on earth before we get to heaven (Micah 6:8; Titus 2:12).

Justification for limited or lethal self-defense for the Christian must be rooted in biblical thought. Argumentation based on natural law, instinct, history, tradition, or the American Constitution is not enough. Like Mary, Jesus's mother, our responses to life situations must be shaped by God's authoritative, eternal, and sufficient word (Luke 1:38; John 2:5).

To that end I want to consider several verses that speak directly or indirectly to the matter of justified self-defense.

Read: Exodus 20:13

Let me begin by looking at the sixth commandment, "You shall not murder." This verse is often quoted on this subject, but for the sake of accuracy and argument it is vitally important we make a distinction between lawful killing and unlawful murdering. Contrary to popular opinion, this commandment is not a prohibition against all killing. The Hebrew term in this case is always associated with unlawful murder. It was never used regarding killing an enemy combatant in war. Why the distinction? Because in God's eyes not all killing is murder. As Kevin D. Zuber notes in *The Moody Bible Commentary*, "Indeed, the OT itself recognizes that there are times when killing in self-defense is not culpable (Ex. 22:2; cf. Est. 9:1–5), when war is necessary (Ex. 17:9), and capital punishment is the appropriate punishment (Gen. 9:6)."[4]

The next time you hear this text quoted remember it is not a blanket prohibition on all killing and is best translated, "You shall not kill unlawfully."

Read: Genesis 14:12-16

In this passage we have an early record of an act of self-defense practiced by Abraham in his attempt to rescue his nephew Lot from the hands of a confederation of four kings. Of note is the fact Abraham is drawn into this armed conflict not over property or possessions but because his relative's life was in peril. Taking 318 armed servants with him, Abraham extricates Lot from danger.

Keeping it plain and simple, this text presents Abraham, the friend of God, as retaining the services of a large group of armed men for the purpose of safeguarding his family and property. Here we have an early canonical record of justified armed self-defense. Abraham defended his immediate and wider family through the threat and use of lethal force. I would assume, because nothing in the text says otherwise, Abraham remained the friend of God despite his expression of armed force in the liberation of Lot.

Read: Exodus 22:1–3

This is a very important text because it comes after the communication of the sixth commandment, which forbids murder (Ex. 20:13). In a section on property rights, we have a clarification given regarding the killing of a thief who breaks into a house in the middle of the night. Remember, under the Mosaic law the taking of a life under certain circumstances is punishable by death (Ex. 21:14). In putting the record straight Moses makes it clear if a man kills an intruder at night not knowing his intention (thief or murderer), the homicide is justifiable in the eyes of God. This is an act of self-defense under ambiguous circumstances, and it does not produce bloodguilt. It is a different situation, however, during the day when the intention of the intruder digging through the walls would be easier to establish. By contrast, to kill a thief when he clearly poses no real threat to life is to become guilty of unlawful bloodshed.

For our purposes, we note this text underscores the lawful and acceptable employment of lethal force in an act of self-defense.

Read: Esther 8:8–9:19

The story of Esther is the story of a hateful and genocidal plot on the part of a man named Haman to destroy the people of God. In a wonderful twist of providence, the Persian King Ahasuerus realizes the deceptive nature and destructive intent of Haman and writes an edict that empowers the Jews within his kingdom to defend themselves against their mortal enemies (Esther 8:11). The King even makes allowance for the Jews to plunder the goods of their defeated enemies. Interestingly the Jews do exercise their right to self-defense, but they do not plunder their enemies, believing it to be a bridge too far.

Again, what we are interested in seeing is it is a given within the biblical text that a person has an innate right to protect himself against anyone who might seek to harm him, his wife, or his children.

Read: Proverbs 24:11 & Psalm 82:4

As these two verses underscore, throughout the Old Testament there is an active call to preserve the life of the innocent and those in mortal danger. As an echo of this principle, we see in the story of the watchman on the wall in Ezekiel 33:1–7 how God promises to hold the watchman guilty if he fails to preserve the life of his fellow citizens by not sounding the alarm. Bottom line, as these texts preach, within the Israelite culture loving one's neighbor naturally extends to protecting them from those who would do them harm (Lev. 19:18).

I think it is fair to conclude and deduce from these verses that rescuing those who are being led away to death will on occasion require lethal force. One would assume deliverance from the wicked will involve a nasty fight. But such an act involving deadly confrontation, is according to the Old Testament, an act of love toward one's neighbor. Neighborliness includes a willingness to act lethally in the defense of those near and dear to us. It is assuredly an act of love to take the life of the wicked to preserve the life of the innocent.

Read: Luke 11:14-22

Moving into the New Testament, we find a similar emphasis on the rightness of self-defense. Here in Luke's gospel we find the Jewish leadership attributing to Jesus the works of Satan. In response, Jesus shows the absurdity of the accusation by noting the blows He inflicted on the kingdom of darkness. If Jesus is on Satan's team, how is He then plundering the kingdom of darkness? Jesus's exorcisms evidently contradict these smears and are proof positive He is stronger than Satan. Jesus is Satan's master, not the other way around.

In making His point, Jesus tells a story of how a robber would have to overpower the owner of a home who is armed and on guard before he could steal any of his stuff. The implication of the story is Jesus would have to be stronger than Satan and attack his kingdom to cast out his demons.

Of interest to us is the fact Jesus' story inherently acknowledges the right to self-defense. He speaks in everyday language of an everyday scene that involves an armed man guarding his house from plunder (Luke 11:21). In a real sense His story is an echo of Moses teaching in Exodus 22:1–3. Consequently, we can conclude both Bible Testaments acknowledge the right of a homeowner to carry a weapon in the cause of protecting home and family.

Read: Luke 22:35–38

This is a key text. For me this text is ground zero in the discussion on Christians, firearms, and self-defense. When Jesus sent his disciples out the first time on mission, He sent them out with nothing in terms of provision or protection. Why? Because He sovereignly arranged for their needs to be meet. The whole thing was a great lesson in trusting God and seeking His kingdom first (Matt. 6:33). However, as Jesus recommissions them for another phase of Gospel ministry, He changes His instruction and encourages His followers to make the necessary practical arrangements for smooth, successful, and safe travels.

Interestingly, He encourages His disciples to sell their cloaks and purchase swords for self-defense (Luke 22:36). The Greek word speaks of a short knife or dagger-like weapon, not a full broadsword, not the doubled-edged sword of Hebrews 4:12. This would be the equivalent to a handgun in our culture. Please bear in mind there was nothing out of the mainstream in Jesus' instruction to His followers to carry a weapon. Life was perilous, and Jesus automatically assumed the right of individuals to protect themselves against wicked and lawless men. After all, carrying a weapon allowed Jesus' disciples to (1) deter the potential for criminality, (2) come to the aid of others who find themselves defenseless, (3) give themselves a fighting chance against stronger attackers, and

(4) compensate for the absence of police and soldiers who cannot be everywhere at once.[5]

Corollary to this, we must note our Lord's condemnation of Peter's use of the sword in Gethsemane is not to be taken as censorship of the right to self-defense as some have proposed (Matt. 26:52). Jesus, as we have shown, assumed the right to self-defense. Rather, what is happening here is Peter was being reprimanded by Christ in his opposing the mob for several distinct reasons:

1. It was a futile act against such a large crowd armed with swords and clubs and would only exacerbate the situation. It was a fight Peter could not win, and his rash actions unnecessarily endangered others.
2. Jesus told His disciples on a number of occasions He was going to Jerusalem to be arrested and killed by the religious leaders of Israel. This was part of God's redemptive plan, and Peter was quite literally fighting it. Peter's rashness stands in contrast to Jesus's submissiveness.
3. By encouraging His disciples to buy swords, Jesus did not mean to imply the sword was a means to be employed either in the propagation or defense of the Gospel. When it comes to missions and ministry, the weapons of our warfare are not physical.

What is clear in this is Jesus is not issuing a blanket condemnation of the use of the sword but a particular condemnation of Peter's improper use. It was the wrong time, occasion, and purpose.

Read: 1 Timothy 5:8

In this text I believe we have an argument for self-defense by natural extension. According to Paul, a godly man and follower of Jesus Christ needs to provide for the welfare of his family. He needs to put a roof over their heads and food in their stomachs. But, is that all? Is his sole concern to be their stomachs? By extension, it must include their emotional health, moral holiness, eternal well-being, and physical safety. What is the point of providing well for his family if the man of the house leaves the house unguarded? Is he to feed his family simply for slaughter? Provision of food is for preservation and preservation naturally includes protection. A man's home is his castle, and as king of that castle he should defend it (Ex. 22:1–3; Neh. 4:13–14; Luke 11:21).

Several pages ago, we set out to defend the right to self-defense from a biblical perspective. I hope in this sampling of verses I have convinced you the Bible does not stutter or stammer on this issue. This is a dangerous world, and every man and woman has God's permission to defend themselves against those who in the normal course of life would seek to rob them of life. There is such a thing as a righteous kill. Not all killing is murder. The right to self-defense may be a constitutional right, but it is a biblical right first.

In his book *52 Weeks with Jesus,* James Merritt tells how, after Christian warriors captured Jerusalem during the First Crusade, pilgrims from all over Europe began flooding into the Holy Land. For their protection, a French knight around AD 1100 formed an organization called the Knights Templar. Their mission was to stand guard over the pilgrims while in the Holy Land. History tell us when these knights were baptized by the church they held their swords above the water while being baptized. It was as if they were saying "Jesus, you can have all of me except this one part. I am all yours except on the battlefield. All I have is yours except my sword"[6]

If I were to make application in the light of our present study, I would remind everyone firearms and their use must be made subject to the Lordship of Jesus Christ. It is His authoritative word that must be allowed to speak the loudest on this issue. Not the Constitution, not our natural inclination, not our family heritage, not our peers. We must let the Bible form and even reform our thinking about firearms and their appropriate use in self-defense. But as we have seen in this chapter, the Bible does speak with authority, clarity, and specificity on this issue, and it does allow for the use of lethal force in defending one's life and home.

THE SAVIOR QUESTION

Was Jesus a pacifist, and did He teach nonresistance in the face of violent assault? A popular vision of Jesus is one in which He is cast as an effeminate kind of figure who pets children on the head, speaks in a soft voice, always repays evil with good, and wouldn't say boo to a fly. This repeated and culturally acceptable caricature of Jesus often emerges from a blurred focus on some of His teaching on the Sermon on the Mount. In the Sermon on the Mount, the Lord Jesus tell His followers to be peacemakers, not to resist the evil person, to go the second mile, to turn the other cheek, to love one's enemies, and to give one's coat to those who want it (Matt. 5–7). Pretty radical stuff and stuff that seems to contradict the notion of taking another's life in the act of self-defense. Given the teaching of Christ in the Sermon on the Mount, might not the Quakers be right that violence must be met with love, forgiveness and nonresistance?

I remember well my first encounter with this kind of interpretation of the Sermon on the Mount. I can recount vividly as a boy listening to my Sunday School teacher tell us about turning the other check, loving your enemies, and how if we were physically attacked we were to put up no resistance. I think my first reaction was, if this is what it means to be a Christian, you can count me out. Given the kind of rough neighborhood I lived in, it all just seemed so unrealistic, foolish, and impractical. To my young ears, that kind of interpretation of Jesus's teaching didn't seem right or just as it allowed for unjust acts to go unchecked. It seemed to further victimize the victim as they were meant to take it on the chin.

But, as the years have gone by, having come to faith in Christ, and studying the Scriptures for myself, I have come to the conviction that to see Jesus in this pacifistic profile and to understand the Sermon on the Mount as a denial of the right to self-defense is misguided.

Let me unpack and clarify some of the more controversial aspects of this discourse and show how they have been misunderstood and twisted to justify pacifism and deny the right to self-defense.

First, it is vital we remember Jesus did not come to destroy the Law or the Prophets but to fulfill them (Matt. 5:17). Jesus often took issue with Rabbinical interpretation of the law but never with the law itself. Jesus never questioned the validity of the law, just its mishandling and misrepresentation by some. After all, Jesus kept it as a Jewish man and fulfilled its symbolism and bore its curse as our Savior. Nowhere in this discourse does Christ subtract from the requirements or relevancy of the law. In fact, the opposite is true. Read the Sermon on the Mount, and you will see Jesus often adds to the law's relevance and significance by reminding His audience the law demands more than mere outward conformity. It is not enough not to murder; one must not harbor anger because murder begins with unfettered anger (Matt. 5:21–25). It is not enough to not commit adultery; one must not lust because for adultery begins with lust (Matt. 5:27–30). As a result, we see the Sermon on the Mount is not in conflict with God's moral law as expressed in the Old Testament.

As it relates to our subject, that means Jesus is not in conflict with the Law as we find it in Exodus where self-protection is sanctioned when there is no other apparent recourse (Ex. 22:2). Whatever the new ethic of Jesus is, it is not at war with God's law. Jesus did not come to destroy the law or the prophets.

Second, it is helpful when looking at the Sermon on the Mount to take into consideration Jesus's clear use of hyperbole. Jesus's employment of overstatement as a means of emphasis is clear to see. He speaks in strong terms, almost extreme terms, to get His point across. Therefore, it would be a mistake to embrace the striking statements of this famous discourse without some qualification. For example, when Jesus speaks about not resisting the evil person, He cannot mean that to apply to all situations at all times because on another occasion He told His disciples to buy swords for self-protection (Matt. 5:39). For another example, when Jesus says to give to him who asks money from you, He cannot mean in an absolute sense for that would mean a beggar could bankrupt any Christian or a church by just asking (Matt. 5:42).

That said, it is very important in looking at several of these texts to see their hyperbolic nature and to be reminded they are not to be embraced without qualification. Jesus's call to express good in the face of evil, grace in the presence of vengeance, and love in the place of hatred must not be taken to mean the suspension of just recompense or the exercise of proper self-defense. To do so would be to dangerously exaggerate Jesus's exaggerated words.

Three, Jesus's call not to retaliate or resist the evil person but to turn the other cheek must be seen for what it is: a call not to aggressively overreact to personal insult (Matt. 5:38–39). This is not a denial of self-protection from assault, but an invitation to show patience and grace in the face of insult and personal belittling. Here Jesus wants us to go the second mile in winning a bad-tempered neighbor to the Gospel. But that is not the same as being called to show nonresistance in the face of a violent assault intended to take one's life unjustly.

In his book *Politics According to the Bible*, Dr. Wayne Grudem has some clarifying words concerning Matthew 5:38–39:

> But Jesus is not prohibiting self-defense here. He is prohibiting individuals from taking personal vengeance simply to 'get even' with another person. The verb "slaps" is the Greek term rhapizo, which refers to a sharp slap given in insult (a right-handed person would use the back of the hand to slap someone on "the right cheek"). So the point is not to hit back when someone hits you as an insult. But the idea of a violent attack to do bodily harm or even murder someone is not in view here.[7]

What is clear is Jesus is not teaching pacifism. Jesus in the Sermon on the Mount nowhere contradicts or removes the right to self-defense in the face of unjust violence. Jesus calls his disciples to be patient, forgiving toward their enemies, kind, and willing to absorb personal insult for the sake of peace, but he does not call them to surrender their lawful right to protect themselves and those they love when justified.

Christian author John Eldredge was shocked and saddened to learn a wicked and infamous drug cartel was requiring its members to read his book *Wild at Heart.* John wrote his book to call men to a renewed commitment to masculinity and to take greater risks for God because God wired men to be spiritual adventurers. And all this is to be done in submission to Christ. But La Familia, a Mexican gang of cold-blooded killers who trafficked in cannabis, used the book in a twisted manner to recruit and train new members. Eldredge, of course was more than upset in hearing this and issued a statement, saying, "It brings me sorrow and anger to know they are doing this, and I renounce their use of my words in this way."[8]

I have often thought about the last part of that statement "I renounce their use of my words in this way" and wondered if Christ might not say that about many a statement made in his name. It is a grave challenge especially to those of us who handle His word on a regular basis and dare to speak in His name. And in the context of our defense of self-defense I cannot help but believe Christ might say those very words to those who take the Sermon on the Mount and mischaracterize Jesus' words to give the impression that in all cases the Christian is to show nonresistance in the face of violence and personal assault.

It is my conviction it is wrong to give people the impression the teachings of the Savior remove their right to self-defense.

THE SOVEREIGNTY QUESTION

Is it a lack of trust in God to own a gun? In reading the material on the issue of self-defense and the possible use of a personal firearm to protect oneself or one's home, some would give the impression security is a matter of trusting God alone. It is stated or implied that it is God's responsibility to protect us, not ours. After all God presents himself in the Scriptures as our strong tower and defense (Prov. 18:10; Psa. 28:7–8). Plus, does the Bible not repeatedly warn against the danger of putting one's trust in military hardware and human resources (Psa. 20:7, 44:6–7).

This emphasis is, I admit, a healthy one. It is good to be reminded often our ultimate security lies with God (Psa. 27:1, 46:1, 90:1). We are indeed prone to shift our trust and find our security in things other than God. That is why it must never be the intention or aim of those defending a person's right to protect themselves to leave anyone trusting in their guns. Our bias must be to cling to God not our guns.

That said, as we pointed out in the last chapter, trusting God does not equate to irresponsibility on our part. God's sovereignty doesn't negate human responsibility. This is true in a broad range of issues. We are to trust God to save the lost, but we still have a responsibly to share the Gospel (Jonah 2:9; Rom. 10:14). We can pray to God for daily bread, but we still have a responsibility to go get a job (Matt. 6:11; 2 Thess. 3:10). And we can ask God to protect us, but we still have a responsibility to take some security steps ourselves (Isa. 26:3; Luke 22:36). We should stay away from dangerous areas, we should lock our doors at night, and as Jesus encouraged His disciples, we should even purchase a weapon.

In relation to this last point, the story of Nehemiah and the rebuilding of the walls of Jerusalem is a classic example of trusting God and yet taking responsibility. Under threat of violence from outside sources, Nehemiah gathers the people of God and tells them on the one hand to remember the Lord and yet on the other hand to fight for their families (Neh. 4:14). Earlier the text records the citizens of Jerusalem prayed to God and at the same time posted armed guards throughout the city (Neh. 4:9). In the actions of Nehemiah and the people of Israel, we have this beautiful balance between trusting God and acting prudently.

This is a balancing act we all need to master. Even the great missionary Hudson Taylor had to learn to balance trust in God with prudent action. During his first voyage to China in 1853, the ship he was traveling on was caught in a violent storm. Facing the possibility of disaster, Taylor refused to wear a life jacket, believing to wear it would be evidence of his lack of trust in God. Later however, he repented of his action believing it to be an obvious mistake. He stated: "The use of means ought not to lessen our faith in God, and our faith in God ought not to hinder our using whatever means He has given us for the accomplishment of his own purposes."[9]

Taking personal responsibility or acting in a practical manner is not incompatible with dependence upon God. Therefore, in the context of our subject I think it is safe to conclude owning a gun is not incompatible with trusting in God. God uses means to fulfill His promise to protect His people, and one of those means might well be a weapon used for self-protection. Surely, the purchase of a fire extinguisher on my part does not mean I don't trust God enough to protect my home, and surely neither does the purchase of a firearm communicate a lack of trust in God either. Both can be used within the providence and rule of God to save lives just like a life-jacket.

As a father of three daughters, I can appreciate the answer basketball hall-of-famer Charles Barkley once gave to a reporter who asked him how he was going to handle the young daughter's future boyfriends. Barkley, tongue in cheek said, "Well, I figure if I shoot the first guy, word will spread."[10]

On a serious note and in closing, the purpose of this chapter has been to spread the word that to fire a shot in self-defense is not forbidden by Scripture, nor is it prohibited by the ethics of Jesus, nor is it incompatible with trusting in God. When discussion takes place on this subject it must ever be remembered the act of self-defense is focused not on taking life but on preserving innocent life. It must be remembered self-defense is not an act of vengeance but rather a just and measured response against evil doers who have no right to expect their lives to come to no harm. Christians can and should take cover in a life guarded by a personal firearm. May this chapter in this book help spread the word it is possible to carry a gun and look like Jesus.

CHAPTER 8

KEEP CALM AND CARRY ON
TAKING COVER IN A LIFE GUARDED BY AN
UNSHAKABLE TRUST IN GOD

Come let us sing the 46th Psalm.

Martin Luther

I am sure you have seen the "Keep Calm and Carry On" shirts, mugs, and posters. They are all the rage. In full disclosure, I have one of the posters on the wall of my study at home. The story behind this fad centers on a motivational poster produced by the British Government shortly after the outbreak of World War II. It was simple and quintessentially British and was intended to be issued upon the expected invasion of Britain by Germany. Its message was designed to raise the morale and eat into the anxiety of the British people. The rallying cry to "Keep Calm and Carry On" was an invitation to bite down on that British stiff upper lip and persevere to victory. Interestingly, while more than two million of them were printed, few saw the light of day. Britain was never invaded, and so the poster was never issued, and most were destroyed or reduced to pulp at the end of the war. However, in 2000, nearly sixty years later, a bookseller in Northumberland, England, stumbled across a copy hidden in a pile of dusty old books bought from an auction. The poster and its reassuring message soon became a commercial sensation.

How do we explain this commercial sensation? Surely, the success of this simple and straightforward slogan in our day testifies to the fact people still seek reassurance in a world riddled with personal tragedy, technological overload, natural disasters, crime, the specter of nuclear war, and the ever-present threat of Islamic terror. The average person on the street wants to know how to keep calm and carry on, they want to live without fear, they want to believe good will triumph over evil, and they want to hope the best is yet to come. Ours is a day and age that desperately needs to be calmed down.

The fact is anxiety disorders are a modern plague in America. While 100% of us worry at some time about something, officially 18% of the US population is in the grip of anxiety. That means nearly 50 million Americans regularly feel the effects of panic attacks, phobias, or other anxiety disorders. As Max Lucado notes in his book *Anxious for Nothing*:

> The land of Stars and Strips has become the country of stress and strife. This is a costly achievement. Stress related ailments cost the nation $300 billion every year in medical bills and lost productivity, while our usage of sedative drugs keeps skyrocketing; just between 1997 and 2004, Americans more than doubled their spending on anti-anxiety medications like Xanax and Valium from $900 million to $2.1 billion . . . As phycologist Robert Leahy points out, "The average child today exhibits the same level of anxiety as the average psychiatric patient in the 1950's."[1]

America needs calming down! As a people, we have allowed anxiety and fear to twist us into emotional pretzels. Our stomachs are in knots, our heads are spinning, our eyes are twitching, our necks are tense, and our souls are unhappy. In fact, there is so much worry going around our nation today those of us who are not worried are starting to worry about the fact we are not worried.

To help us "Keep Calm and Carry On," I want to turn our attention to Psalm 46. This psalm was written out of a context of impending disaster and national peril, and yet we see the people of Israel remain fearless; they were able to remain calm and carry on, all because the Lord of hosts was with them and the God of Jacob was their refuge (Psa. 46:7, 11). In the face of great anxiety, they put their trust in God and experienced the hush of heaven within their hearts (Psa. 46:10). They were able to fortify their shivering souls against wintery fear by taking refuge in God (Psa. 46:1). They calmed down by looking up.

Psalm 46 is one of several Psalms molded around the theme of confidence in God. In the world of biblical scholarship, they are known as songs of trust; each is an affirmation of faith in God. They teach and preach the unfailing nature of God's character, the history of His works of providence, the value of trusting Him, and the danger of trusting anything or anyone else. Psalm 23 is probably the best known in this group, but others include Psalm 11, 27, 62, 63, 90, 91, and 121. Like these other songs of trust, Psalm 46 exudes this unshakable confidence in God in the face of monstrous crisis and earthshattering circumstances. The message of a song of trust is that God's people can be calm because as God's people they can be confident and because their confidence lies in their glorious, sovereign, loving, merciful, faithful God. Omnipotence is working for them.

As an expression of trust in God, this psalm was probably written during a time of war and national insecurity. As best we can tell, Psalm 46 was authored to celebrate Israel's divine deliverance from the invading Assyrians under King Sennacherib (around 701 BC). In the span of one evening, as Jerusalem was surrounded by Assyrians soldiers baying for blood, God answered the desperate prayer of King Hezekiah through the mouth of the prophet Isaiah and sent an angel through the camp of the Assyrians, killing some 185,000 men. By dawn the remaining Assyrians had fled out of fear (2 Kings 19:35–36; Isa. 37:33–37; Psa. 46:5). Psalm 46 is a celebration of that startling story.

While this song was written for an ancient audience in different times, it still speaks to our day. Ours is also a day when nations rage and kingdoms are moved (Psa. 46:6). The Middle East continues to be a tinder box, Europe is reeling from an invasion of migrants and refugees from Africa and the Middle East, Russia is invading her neighbors, Iran is in search of a nuclear weapon with the express purpose of destroying Israel, and America is in a protracted war against Islamic Jihadism. Adding to these, the average person is fighting his own battles with spiritual struggles, emotional hang-ups, limited finances, family disputes, deteriorating health, troubled neighborhoods, and fears about the future.

Christians in particular are concerned about the plight of Israel, growing persecution around the world, a changing moral landscape, and the fact we look to be entering a post-Christian era. By any measure, the tide seems to be turning against all we consider sacred.

These are indeed unsettling and uncertain times, but that makes Psalm 46 all the more relevant. This sweet song, this celebration of God's past works, sets before us the promise of the presence of God as an ever-present help to God's people. That is why, during the upheaval and strain of the Protestant Reformation in Europe Martin Luther, the great German reformer, would often say to his family and friends at moments of mounting stress, "Come let us sing the 46th Psalm."

In digging into this psalm, we are returning to a theme I introduced in my introduction. My years with the police in Northern Ireland taught me security is not the absence of danger but the presence of God in the midst of danger. Psalm 46 shows us security is not the absence of danger but the presence of God (Psa. 46:1–3, 5, 7, 10, 11). Sometimes God calms the storm, but most of the time God calms His children in the midst of the storm by reminding them He is in the boat with them. Remember the story in the Gospels when Jesus calms the storm and how the disciples needed to learn afresh to focus on who was in the boat with them and not what was going on outside the boat (Mark 4:35–41). They forgot the wind and the waves obey Christ. Peace is not finding a sea where there are no squalls or storms; peace is knowing God is onboard your life and has His hand on the tiller of history.

As we study this psalm there are three stanzas to this song:

1. The Refuge (vv. 1–3)
2. The River (vv. 4–7)
3. The Rest (vv. 8–11)

THE REFUGE

If we accept that the siege of Jerusalem by Sennacherib is the historical backdrop to the writing of this psalm, then this was certainly a time of national upheaval and upset. The air was thick with apprehension. The invasion from the north by this world super power was nothing less than a political earthquake. Among the citizens of Jerusalem and those in power, there was little sense of safety. The outcome of the siege was uncertain, the future of the nation unknown, and everything about life was in flux. This was a 9/11-type event within Israel.

The tension and sense of dread among the inhabitants of Jerusalem was so deep and wide, King Hezekiah makes reference to the fact pregnant women about to give birth were lacking the will to deliver their babies (2 Kings 19:3).

In Psalm 46, the language of natural disaster is employed to convey the political upheaval and sense of national peril felt throughout the land. Politically and nationally, Israel was experiencing a category 5 hurricane (Psa. 46:1–3, 6). In the Bible, *mountains* can speak of empires and *waters* can speak of nations. These images of upheaval address the fact their world was being shaken and stirred by the invading Assyrians. Mountains sliding into the sea and waves crashing against the coast illustrate chaos and calamity.

But during all this upset and upheaval, there was a safe space and refuge for the people of God. That refuge was Israel's ever-present God

(Psa. 46:1; 18:1–2; 91:1–4). There was no need for the people of God to fear, for God remained unmoved despite all the commotion and chaos. By faith they could embrace the reality there was no panic in heaven, only plans. The Holy Trinity, Father, Son, and Holy Spirit, did not rush to hold emergency talks on how to handle the breaking news. God was not threatened, nor was His throne shaken by the mayhem surrounding the city of Jerusalem (Psa. 2:1–4; 115:1–3). The angels of heaven went about their business with a calm assurance. Heaven's streets continued to be suffused with a sweet and sacred serenity.

The citizens of Jerusalem and King Hezekiah could turn to God and find Him to be a shelter in a time of storm and an impenetrable stronghold in battle. He was to them a sanctuary and stronghold (Psa. 46:1). God's name and all it promises was to them a strong tower to run into and feel safe (Prov. 18:10; Psa. 77:7).

A couple years back, I made a visit home to see my parents in Northern Ireland. While there I decided to go see Carrickfergus Castle, a Norman fortification within Ireland just north of Belfast, built by Sir John De Courcy several centuries ago. Although I had been before, I hadn't been for some time, so I thought it was time for a revisit. As a typical castle of its times, it had large stone walls as its outer defenses. Along the walls, canons were strategically placed. But inside the castle, there was what was called the "keep" or the "stronghold." This was really a small castle within the castle where the walls were thickest and windows and doors fewest, and it was the place for a desperate last stand should the outer defenses be breached. While taking in all the sights, sounds, and smells of that ancient fortification, I was reminded how God is my strong tower, my keep, and my refuge. God's kingdom has never been conquered. His rule and reign has never been overturned; He is to His people a refuge and stronghold in all generations (Psa. 90:1–2; 102:25–28). God is by nature immutable and unassailable (Mal. 3:6; Heb. 13:5–8). His word stands forever, His love is steadfast, His mercy unfailing, His powerful presence constant.

In a world constantly turning and churning, it is great to be able, like the citizens of Jerusalem at the time of King Hezekiah and like the saints across history, to run to God for peace and protection. To hide by His side. To find as mentioned earlier, His name as a strong tower and to run into it and feel safe (Prov. 18:10). What refuge and strength we can find as God's people in mediating on God's name and trusting God to be to us what His name [or names] promises.

Think about the names of God. God is:

- Jehovah-Ra'ah: The Lord, my Shepherd (Psa. 23:1)
- Jehovah-Jireh: The Lord, my provider (Gen. 22:14)
- Jehovah-Shalom: The Lord, my peace (Judges 6:24)
- Jehovah-Rapha: The Lord, my healer (Ex. 15:26)
- Jehovah-Tsidkenu: The Lord, my righteousness (Jer. 23:6)
- Jehovah-Shammah: The Lord, ever-present (Ezek. 48:35)
- Jehovah-Nissi: The Lord, our banner (Ex. 17:15)[2]

How wonderful! God is all these things, all the time for His people. These truths about God's character and commitments act like walls around our hearts when we face the onslaught of worry, fear, and anxiety. His peace guards us (Phil. 4:6–7). With God as our refuge, with omnipotence working for us, we need not fear even though things may be tumbling in all around us (Psa. 46:1–3). The God who is, who was, and who is to come is our stronghold in all the changes and challenges that make up our lives (Rev. 1:8). We take refuge in the fact espoused by C. H. Spurgeon when he said:

> *The Christian knows no change with regard to God. He may be rich today and poor tomorrow; he may be sickly today and well tomorrow; he may be in happiness today, tomorrow he may be distressed; but there is no change with regard to his relationship to God. If he loved me yesterday he loves me today, I am neither better nor worse in God than I ever was. Let prospects be blighted, let hopes be blasted, let joy be withered, let mildews destroy everything. I have lost nothing of what I have in God.*

How true. God is our refuge in all generations. Changes within history, changes within life, and changes within you or me do not change Him. You can take the promise of His inseparable love, unerring wisdom, amazing grace, constant faithfulness, and long patience to the bank. God stands amidst the rumble and ruin of life like an impenetrable tower providing safety and security for those who trust in Him.

Walter Winchell was a well-known and respected radio news commentator during World War II. Once, after a particularly dark week during which the port of Singapore fell to the Japanese, he closed his broadcast with this memorable line: "Singapore has fallen but the Rock of Ages stands."[3]

There are times when it feels as though our world is falling apart. That was certainly how the inhabitants of Jerusalem felt as the Assyrians surrounded their city. God is to us a "very present help in time of trouble" (Psa. 46:1). Interestingly, the phrase "very present help" can be translated "help from of old." Fits well with what I am saying. God is the same help yesterday, today, and forever.

THE RIVER

God is not only a refuge, He is also a river (Psa. 46:4–6). One of the things not to be missed within Psalm 46 is the compelling contrast the author sets up between the roaring waters and the flowing river. The roaring waters is a picture of the invading Assyrians swamping the city of Jerusalem with the threat of death and disaster (Psa. 46:3, 6). The flowing river is a picture of God supplying grace to the people of God under great pressure (Psa. 46:4–5). There is water that rattles the people of God, and there is water that refreshes the people of God.

In his usage of the image of a river, I believe the author of this religious poem is connecting some historical dots and is probably referring to the building of Hezekiah's tunnel (2 Chron. 32:2–4, 30; 2 Kings 20:20). In preparation for the impending siege of Jerusalem by the Assyrians, King Hezekiah undertook an engineering marvel for that time by excavating a channel through solid rock so the Gihon Spring outside the city could supply water to inside the city. The conduit was roughly 1,770 feet long, was started on both ends of the project simultaneously, and miraculously met in the middle. Upon completion of the tunnel, all outside traces of the Gihon Spring were covered. The Assyrians outside had no idea of the water supply under the walls of Jerusalem making glad the hearts of the people. This secret supply was key to the city's survival.

Let us not forget Jerusalem as a capital city at that time was a very unusual city because it had no natural water supply, which consequently made it very susceptible to capture. Rome had the Tiber, Babylon had the Euphrates, Nineveh had the Tigris, Egyptian cities had the Nile, and Damascus had the Barada. All Jerusalem had was the Gihon spring outside the city.[4]

Theologically however, we must look beyond the Gihon spring and conclude the psalmist is deliberately piggy-backing on the historic story of Hezekiah's tunnel to remind the people of God the real river in the midst of the beleaguered inhabitants of the Jerusalem was God. Just as Hezekiah's tunnel supplied life-giving water to the city, so God's presence in Jerusalem was a stream of never-failing mercy (Psa. 46:3–5). Remember God's presence and provision, God's glory and grace, are often pictured in the Bible in terms of a flowing river (Gen. 2:10–13; Ezek. 47:1–12; Rev. 22:1–2). In the context of Psalm 46, the river that brought joy to the people of God was God's abiding and abundant presence. God was a river of delights to His people. The seething waters of Assyrians' aggression were no match for the citizens of Jerusalem who drew their strength and refreshment from God's ever flowing love, peace, and grace (Jer. 2:13; John 7:37–39).

I love it! When the chips are down, when the problems pile up, when the shadows gather, when the barbarians are at the gates, God's people can drink from the well of salvation (Isa. 12:3; 49:10; Psa. 23:5). God is to His people an artesian well of grace giving, an ever-flowing source of life.

This thought is wonderfully captured in John Gospel as he speaks of Jesus's life and ministry and "of His fullness we have all received grace for grace" (John 1:16). The idea behind "grace for grace" is "grace instead of grace" or "grace in the place of grace." What a beautiful picture of a perpetual succession of grace. God's favor piled on top of God's favor. A ceaseless loop of demand and supply, our demands and needs being met by God's gracious supply of grace and peace. In fact, nobody captures the power and poignancy of this picture better than Bishop Handley Moule of England as he writes:

> *The picture before us is as of a river. Stand on its banks and contemplate the flow of waters. A minute passes, and another. Is it the same stream still? Yes. But is it the same water? No. The liquid mass that passed you seconds ago fills now another section of the channel; new water has displaced it, or if you please replaced it; water instead of water. And so, hour by hour, and year by year, and century by century, the process holds; one stream, other waters, living not stagnant, because in the great identity there is perpetual exchange. Grace takes the place of grace; (Love takes the place of love) ever new, ever old, ever the same, ever fresh and young, for hour by hour, for year by year through Christ.[5]*

Life may be exacting and exhausting, but the child of God, just like the inhabitants of Jerusalem under Hezekiah, has an inexhaustible supply of God's grace (2 Cor. 9:8; 1 Pet. 5:10). Whatever our need, God has a portion of grace suited and tailored for our time of need (Heb. 4:14–16). There is saving grace for our sin (Eph. 2:8–10), singing grace for our sorrows (Col. 3:16), sufficient grace for our trials (2 Cor. 12:1–9), speaking grace for our opportunities (Col. 4:6), and strengthening grace for our weaknesses (2 Tim. 2:1). There is grace in the place of grace.

Rowland Hill was a contemporary of C. H. Spurgeon in London and was given a large sum of money to dispense to a poor pastor working elsewhere in the city. Thinking the money was too much to send all at once and the brother might be better served by receiving it in portions, Rowland Hill dolled it out bit by bit over time. Interestingly, every time he sent the man some money through the post, he would include this note in the envelope, "More to follow."

C. H. Spurgeon used to borrow that story and apply it to God's good giving to His people. He would say, "Every blessing that comes from God is sent with the same message, 'And more to follow.' 'I forgive you your sins, but more to follow.' 'I justify you in the righteousness of Christ, but there is more to follow.' 'I adopted you into my family, but there is more to follow.' 'I educated you for heaven, but there is more to follow.' 'I give you grace upon grace, but there is more to follow.' 'I have helped you even to old age, but there is more to follow.' 'I will uphold you in the hour of death and as you are passing into the world of the spirits, my mercy shall still continue with you, and when you land in the world to come there shall still be more to follow.'"[6]

Wow! When life drains us of our resolve, empties us of our hope, and subtracts from the number our days on earth, we need to keep a firm grip on the fact that with God there is always more to follow. He is to those who put their trust in Him through Christ a never-ending stream of mercy, love, and grace.

THE REST

The focus of the final stanza in this psalm moves us beyond the immediate political and military situation in Jerusalem in 701 BC to a moment in the future when God will bring an end to the hostilities between men and between men and God (Psa. 46:8–11). The remaining verses of this song are particularly addressed to God's enemies. The psalmist pronounces there is coming a day when God will be exalted among the nations. The Lord of angel armies who has triumphed within history, as recorded in the stories of the Exodus, the defeat of the Assyrians, and the humbling of Nebuchadnezzar, will someday triumph manifestly at the end of history (Psa. 46:8–9, 10). Those who oppose the rule of God, those who hurt the people of God, those who blaspheme the Son of God will face desolation and destruction. Under God's visible rule on earth through the Lord Jesus Christ, war will give way to peace, blasphemy give way to worship, hostility give way to harmony, and man's mismanagement give way to God's glorious rule (Psa. 2; Rev. 19–22).

Every defeat within history of a hostile power opposed to God, His Son, His people, and His kingdom is a window into God's plans for mankind. God is committed to the removal in the end of every evil instigator, bad actor, and godless nation opposed to His rule on earth. God in an act of judgment is going to make a clean sweep of sin. As Derek Kidner notes, "Although the outcome is peace the process is judgment."[7] There is an apocalypse coming; within history it will get worse before it gets better. There is a divine storm that will rain wrath on a rebellious planet before the final calm (Isa. 9:5; Dan. 12:1; 2 Peter 3:12ff).

While we tend to personalize Psalm 46:10, it is better within the context of this psalm to see it primarily as a call to the nations to submit to God's sovereign rule. God is summoning the leaders and inhabitants of this world to lay down their arms, to cease and desist their opposition to His will and Son. It is an edict from the high king of heaven to stop fighting and acknowledge His authority over life (Isa. 2:4; 11:4, Zech. 9:10; Rev. 11:15; 20:1–10). Just as Jesus commanded the wind and the waves to be still, to lie down, so God will call the nations of this world to acknowledge at the end of history what they have failed to acknowledge within history; He is God and His Son is Lord (Phil. 2:9–11).

In the meantime, God's people can still their own hearts by putting their trust in the Sovereign God, One who is the Lord of human history, and who someday will be exalted among the nations (Eph. 1:11; Rom. 11:36). According to the Bible, man's mismanagement and Satan's pillaging of the planet will come to an end. Therefore, the Christian's sense of security in a world at war with God and itself is to be found in the coming of the Prince of Peace (Isa. 9:6–7). The sure promise of peace on earth through the judgment of God and the reign of Christ is the thing that brings present day peace to our troubled hearts (John 14:27; Isa. 26:3). The anxious soul and troubled Christian is to rest in the hope of Jesus's return and to keep on trusting God in their immediate circumstances (2 Thess. 1:3–10). We can remain calm in the knowledge that someday soon God will tell this rebellious and restless world to be still, to lie down, or better still to bow down (Psa. 46:10). It is this prospect and perspective that allows us to hope, take courage, keep our balance, steady our nerves, and look beyond our present problems with a cheery disposition.

I love the story told by missionary Gregory Fisher. Fisher was teaching a class at the West African Bible College when he was caught off guard by a question posed to him by one of his students. The student asked, "What will He say when He shouts?" The question emerged from the student's study of 1 Thessalonians 4:16 where he read of Jesus's return for His people and the fact Jesus would come down from heaven with a shout. The student was interested to know the professors take on what Jesus would shout.

Fisher thought about side stepping the question by reminding the student that when the Bible is silent we should leave off our inquiries. If God wanted us to know something He would have made it clear. But Fisher's mind took him back to a conversation earlier in the day with a refugee from the Liberian civil war.

The man who was a high school principal told of how he escaped a death squad. After hiding in the bush for two days, he gathered his family and fled to a neighboring country. But the path to freedom and safety was a painful one with the loss of two of his children along the way.

Alongside that experience, Fisher observed beggars along the route to his office. He was troubled afresh by the indignity heaped on these people reduced to beggary. He continued to be haunted by the vacant eyes of people who lost all hope.

Given the events and the experiences of the day, Fisher decided not to dodge the question. Turning to the student who asked the question he said, "He will shout 'enough!' When Jesus returns He will shout 'enough!'"

A look of surprise covered the face of the student, "What do you mean, enough?"

The professor replied, "Enough suffering. Enough starvation. Enough terror. Enough death. Enough indignity. Enough lives trapped in hopelessness. Enough sickness and disease. Enough time. Enough!"[8]

That will indeed be a glorious and long-awaited day when Jesus shouts "Enough!" Enough division, despair, death, disease, and enough of the devil. This is our hope, and it is a hope big enough to keep us strong in our faith, sure in our hope, and resolute in our love.

In drawing the curtain on this chapter and this book, we have been reminded once again that security is not the absence of danger but the presence of God. God is a help in trouble not an escape from it. God is in life's most difficult circumstances supplying the grace we need to overcome. And God tells us to be at peace as we await the Prince of Peace.

Take cover in a life guarded by an unshakable trust in God. With the protestant reformer Martin Luther and the saints of old come let us sing Psalm 46. John Wesley was right, "Best of all God is with us!"

ACKNOWLEDGMENTS

The Christian teacher and author A. W. Tozer once said, "The only book that should ever be written is the one that flows from the heart, forced out by inward pressure." *Take Cover* is a book I hope meets that criteria. First, this is a book I have written out of my own personal experience. Growing up and serving as a police officer during the Troubles in Northern Ireland forced me and taught me to take cover in God's promises and protections. Second, this is a book I have written out my own pastoral experience as I have watched hurting people find God to be their refuge and strength during times of trouble.

No author is an island, and so I want to express my deep gratitude to a number of people for making this project possible. First and foremost, I wish to thank the leadership and congregation of Kindred Community Church for their constant prayers, love, and support. The basic outline of this book was first presented to Kindred as a sermon series and was warmly received. Kindred Community Church allows me to do my ministry with joy and not grief. What a blessing from God!

Alongside the church, I am appreciative of the team at our national radio ministry "Know the Truth" and the partnership we have in the Gospel. You have encouraged me to write, and your heart for helping people through the Word has inspired me to write. Among that team, I want to especially thank Matt Thomas for his friendship and friendly nudges to finish the project.

To the good folks at Salem Books, I also say thank you. Your trust in me, your counsel to me, and your leadership throughout this project have made this book possible. A special shout goes to Gary Terashita for his helpful suggestions and excellent editing throughout the writing of this manuscript. Thank you for correcting and smoothing out my Irish English.

Last but certainly not least, I continue to be indebted to my wife June whose support has allowed me to flourish in all aspects of my ministry, whose love inspires me on a daily basis, and whose selflessness allows me to find the extra time to write.

Because all things are from God and to God I finish by acknowledging that I am what I am, simply and solely, by the grace of God. When it comes to the writing of Take Cover, to God be the glory!

Philip De Courcy
Anaheim Hills, California

ENDNOTES

INTRODUCTION

1. Warren Wiersbe, *Turning Mountains into Molehills,* (Grand Rapids, MI: Baker Book House, 1973) 135.
2. Steve Brown, *Jumping Hurdles,* (Grand Rapids, MI: Baker Books, 1992) 62.
3. John Pollock, *A Fistful of Heroes*, (Ross-shire, UK: Christian Focus Publications, 1998) 104.
4. R. Kent Hughes, *1001 Great Stories & Quotes*, (Wheaton, IL: Tyndale House Publishers Inc., 1998) 84.

CHAPTER 1

1. David Jeremiah, *Turning Toward Joy,* (Wheaton, IL: Victor Books, 1992), 170.
2. Michael Green, *Illustrations for Biblical Preaching,* (Grand Rapids, MI: Baker Book House, 1989), 407.
3. inclair B. Ferguson, *Let's Study Philippians*, (Edinburgh, Scotland: The Banner of Truth Trust, 1997), 104.
4. Leonard Griffiths, *This Is Living*, (Cambridge, United Kingdom: Lutterworth Press,).
5. J. H. Pickford, *Paul's Spiritual Biography,* (London, England: Marshall, Morgan, and Scott, Ltd, 1949), 110-111.
6. J. C. Ryle, *The Five English Reformers*, (Carlisle, PA: Banner of Truth Trust, 1981) 11.

CHAPTER 2

1. Phil Moore, *Psalms*, (Grand Rapids, MI: Monarch Books, 2013), 140.
2. Joni Eareckson Tada, *A Lifetime of Wisdom*, (Grand Rapids, MI: Zondervan, 2009), 38.
3. Sam Storms, *More Precious than Gold*, (Wheaton, IL: Crossway Books, 2009) 156.
4. Danny Akin, *10 Who Changed the World*, (Nashville, TN: B&H Publishing Group, 2012), 24.
5. Warren Wiersbe, *With the Word*, (Nashville, TN: Thomas Nelson, 1991), 355.
6. Ray Galea, *God is Enough,* (Kingsford, New South Wales: Matthias Media, 2010), 147.
7. Derek Tidball, *Signposts: A Devotional Map of the Psalms,* (Nottingham, England: IVP, 2009), Psalm 73.

CHAPTER 3

1. Gregory C. Cochran, *Christians in the Crosshairs,* (Wooster, OH: Weaver Book Company, 2016), 23.
2. John Maxwell, *On This Holy Night,* (Nashville TN: Thomas Nelson, 2013), 2.
3. John Blanchard, *Gathered Gold*, (Hertfordshire, England: Evangelical Press, 1984), 319.
4. Victor Kuligin, *Ten Things I Wish Jesus Never Said*, (Wheaton, IL: Crossway Books, 2006), 119.
5. Tim Chester, *The Ordinary Hero*, (Nottingham, England: IVP, 2009), 207–8.
6. Michelle DeRusha, *50 Women Every Christian Should Know*, (Grand Rapids, MI: Baker Books, 2014), 278.
7. Warren Wiersbe, *Walking with the Giants*, (Grand Rapids, MI: Baker Book House, 1971), 61.

CHAPTER 4

1. Roy B. Zuck, *Devotions for Kindred Spirits*, (Wheaton, IL: Victor Books, 1990), 275.
2. David Roper, *Seeing Through*, (Sisters, OR: Multnomah Books, 1995), 24.
3. Phil Moore, *John*, (Grand Rapids, MI: Monarch Books, 2012), 221.
4. Dr. Jim Rosscup, *An Exposition of Prayer, New Testament Volume 2*, (Chattanooga, TN: AMG Publishers, 2011), 2169.
5. Max Anders, *The Good Life*, (Dallas, TX: Word Publishing 1993), 285.

CHAPTER 5

1. Ray Stedman, *God's Final Word*, (Grand Rapids MI: Discovery House Publishers, 1991), 2.
2. Mark Hitchcock, *101 Answers to the Most Asked Questions about the End Times*, (Sisters, OR: Multnomah Publishers, 2001), 89.
3. To further study the doctrine of the Rapture read *Can We Still believe in the Rapture?* by Ed Hindson and Mark Hitchcock.
4. Thomas Ice & Timothy Demy, *Prophecy Watch*, (Eugene, OR: Harvest House Publishers, 1998), 10.
5. David Jeremiah, *Jesus Final Warning*, (Nashville, TN: Word Publishing, 1999), 73.

CHAPTER 6

1. Brian Harbour, *Rising Above the Crowd*, (Nashville, TN: Broadman Press, 1988), 63.
2. John MacArthur, *Why Government Can't Save You*, (Nashville, TN: Word Publishing, 2000), 27.
3. Erwin Lutzer, *Hitler's Cross*, (Chicago, IL: Moody Publishers, 2012), 121.

4. Editor: Craig Brian Larson, *Illustrations for Preaching and Teaching,* (Grand Rapids, MI: Baker Books, 1993), 257.

5. Michael Reagan, *In the Words of Ronald Reagan*, (Nashville, TN: Nelson Books, 2004), 115.

6. Editor: Craig Brian Larson, *Contemporary Illustrations for Preachers, Teachers, and Writers,* (Grand Rapids, MI: Baker Books, 1996), 92.

7. Editors: Wayne Martindale and Jerry Root, *The Quotable C. S. Lewis,* (Wheaton, IL: Tyndale House Publishers, Inc. 1989), 271.

8. Wayne Grudem, *Politics According to the Bible,* (Grand Rapids, MI: Zondervan, 2010), 80.

9. Paul Schlehlein, *John G. Paton, Missionary to the Cannibals of the South Seas,* (Carlisle, PA: The Banner of Truth Trust, 2018) 46–48.

CHAPTER 7

1. David O. Dykes, *Ten Requirements for American Survival,* (Maitland, FL: Xulon Press, 2004), 77.

2. Wayne Grudem, *Politics According to the Bible,* (Grand Rapids, MI: Zondervan, 2010), 208.

3. Charles Dyer & Mark Tobey, *The Isis Crisis,* (Chicago, IL: Moody Press, 2013), 128.

4. General Editors: Michael Rydelnik & Michael Vanlaningham, *The Moody Bible Commentary,* (Chicago, IL: Moody Publishers, 2014), 142.

5. Ibid., Grudem, 203.

6. James Merritt, *52 Weeks with Jesus,* (Eugene, OR: Harvest House Publishers, 2014) 195.

7. Ibid., Grudem 202.

8. Steven D. Mathewson, *Preaching the Four Gospels with Confidence,* (Peabody, MA: Hendrickson Publishers, 2013), 109.

9. Nickey Gumbel, *Challenging Lifestyle,* (Eastbourne, England: Kingsway Publications, 1996), 190.

10. Stephen Davey, *Titus,* (Apex, NC: Charity House Publishers, 2015), 65.

CHAPTER 8

1. Max Lucado, *Anxious for Nothing,* (Nashville, TN: Thomas Nelson, 2017), 6.

2. Adrian Rogers, *The Lord Is My Shepherd,* (Wheaton, IL: Crossway Books, 1999), 22.

3. Powell W. Powell, *Death from the Other Side,* (Nashville, TN: Annuity Board of the SBC, 1991), 46.

4. Phil Moore, *Psalms,* (Grand Rapids, MI: Monarch Books, 2013), 105.

5. Elizabeth Skoglund, *Wounded Heroes,* (Grand Rapids, MI: Baker Book House, 1992), 60.

6. Charles Spurgeon, *The Quotable Spurgeon,* (Wheaton IL: Harold Shaw Publishers, 1990), 89.

7. Derek Kidner, *Psalm 1–72,* (Downers Grove, IL: IVP, 1973), 176.

8. Craig Brian Larson, *Illustrations for Preaching & Teaching,* (Grand Rapids, MI: Baker Books, 1993), 210.